LIVING WITHOUT THEM

My Journey with Loss

REV. DR. JOSÉ H. TATE

Mom and Me

CONTENT

ACKNOWLEDGMENTS

The thoughts and words within this book are dedicated to my father, mother, grandfather, grandmother, four brothers, aunt, niece, sister-in-law, and father-in-law who've all gone on before me. Through the years, one by one, my family members lived and left their unique mark upon those of us who loved them. They may be gone, but they will never be forgotten.

INTRODUCTION

As human beings, we come from different backgrounds and have different stories. Yet, we share similar life experiences. One experience we share is the loss of a loved one. Of course, losing a loved one can be very difficult. For me, my toughest losses occurred when I lost family members. Although many of us have challenges within our families, family can be instrumental in our growth and development. Family can give us a sense of belonging and security, and family can help us understand who we are. And there are certain family members whose love seems hard to replace. If family and loved ones are hard to replace, what happens to us when they're gone?

Some family members, like my grandfather and aunt, left me when I was very young. Although stories of their lives and pictures help fill in the blank spaces of not knowing them very well, I missed what we might have shared. I miss the love, joy, and strength they would have given me, and the wisdom and life experiences they would have added to my life. Though they haven't been around for a very long time, I'm determined to keep them in my heart.

Some family members, like my father and mother, left me when I was entering adulthood. I didn't need any pictures or stories to fill blank spaces concerning them. I knew and loved them very well. My mom and dad were the backbone of my family. Together, they were a pretty good team. I miss that team. Although my mom and dad were gone before my twenty-third birthday, I can still see their smiling faces, hear their laughter, and feel their love. I wish they hadn't left me so soon. Yet, even today, their lives still speak to me.

Other family members—my brothers, grandmother, sister-in-law, and niece—passed away during my young adult to middle-aged years.

Needless to say, the journey wasn't always easy. Yet, God never said that life would be easy or that we would never experience loss or pain. He said He would be with us and never leave us; give us comfort and strength; bring healing in our lives; and transform our pain—if we let Him. To this end, God has helped change my perspective about suffering and loss to a more hopeful and empowering one. Today, I thank God for giving me those I've lost instead of feeling victimized as a result of losing them. Often I remind myself that God is in control of life and death, not me. I can only control the things I can control and leave the rest in God's hands. Therefore, I can choose to continue to love and celebrate my departed loved ones and live a life that would honor their memory. Does this mean I don't miss them or fight the temptation to linger on their absence? No. It means I don't have to stay or live in a state of bereavement. Through Christ, I have hope. Since God is able to wipe away our tears, bring healing to our hearts, and turn one's negatives into positives, I'm encouraged! "Living Without Them" may mean our departed loved ones are physically absent, but their life and influence can forever live through us.

The Way It Was – growing up

It seemed like family and loss would make its mark on my life from the very beginning. In the early 1960s, my biological mother (and father) gave me up for adoption. Soon, I would become part of the Tate family—I entered the home as a baby and was later officially adopted. If I were to highlight some of the major themes in my early life as they relate to family and loss, they would be I lost a family; I gained a family; I loved and lived with this family in a challenging environment; then, I lost again—the greatest loss of my life. This is the way it was. In spite of those challenges, or perhaps because of them, God would use those years to prepare me for adulthood. I would need those lessons as I moved through the stages of my life.

I LOST A FAMILY AND GAINED A FAMILY

Adoption is sort of a mixed bag when it comes to how it may affect one's life. On the one hand, adoption can be seen as positive, with potential and promise for the future. The act of adoption is significant in the sense that an individual or a couple intentionally picks a baby or child from the masses to become a new member of their family. Usually, adoptive parents have to meet certain criteria to be eligible to adopt children. So, potentially, adoptive parents may offer a better life and unique opportunities for the adopted child than could be afforded the child remaining in an unwanted situation.

When I think of the positive features and potential gains of adoption, I'm reminded of God's great love in adopting "lost souls" into His fold. In the Bible (all Scriptures are from the New King James Version), Ephesians 1:5–8, the Apostle Paul tells believers at Ephesus that God "predestined us to adoption as sons by Jesus Christ to Himself, according to the good pleasure of His will, to the praise of the glory of His grace, by which He made us accepted in the Beloved. In Him we have redemption through His blood, the forgiveness of sins, according to the riches of His grace which He made to abound toward us in all wisdom and prudence." In another Scripture, Romans 8:14–15, the Apostle Paul tells believers at Rome, "For as many as are led by the Spirit of God, these are the sons of God. For you did not receive the spirit of bondage again to fear, but you received the Spirit of adoption by whom we cry out, 'Abba, Father.'"

In these examples, one can see the condition of a person before and after being adopted by a loving Father (God). Before adoption, one is in spiritual bondage, limited, and separated from the one who offers security, love, meaning, purpose, and life. Yet after adoption, one's life and opportunities for love, fulfillment, wholeness, and feeling connected are suddenly possible. On the positive, as God offers new life and possibilities to those adopted into His family, adoptive parents might offer a better life and new possibilities for the precious child.

I must say I appreciate having adoption—a situation with possibilities and promise—as an alternative to growing up unwanted in a birth home. Adoptions not only give adoptees a new name, but new people eager to share their love and life with them. I would count myself in the number of adoptees who found love and acceptance within my adoptive family—the only family I've ever known.

Mom and Dad were in their mid-forties when I entered the Tate home. When I was a child, Dad, a WWII veteran, worked for the city, and Mom was a maid. Dad was what I would call a "meat and potatoes" man. He was a solid citizen, hardworking, strong, and a man who cared for his family. He rarely argued or complained, and he didn't mingle with a lot of people—although he was friendly. Mom was the quintessential mother. She was religious, kind, caring, humble, and pleasant to everyone she met. Mom was the kind of mother who would feed a stranger, clothe the naked, and reach out to the poor and disenfranchised. In fact, she probably was kind to a fault because she (and my dad) spoiled my brothers and me—although I'll take being spoiled over being abandoned any day of the week.

Although both parents loved me, I must admit, I was the apple of my mother's eye. I always knew that if others failed me or had little use for me, Mom would never give up on me. For better or worse, I was her son. I cannot recall one moment or incident when she wavered in her devotion toward me. I was blessed to have her for a mother. As I reflect upon her love, I believe Mom gave me a glimpse of God's love. With Mom, I could find acceptance, grace, mercy, charity, and support. Dad's love was a little more human. His love and support were sure, but Dad's love didn't seem as large and wide as Mom's. Still, I was fortunate to have both of these individuals in my life. While these individuals were in my life, they never made me feel like I was less than a son, and I never looked at them in any other way than mother and father. This aspect of adoption positively redefined my life.

On the other hand, through adoption, a child experiences his or her first loss—the loss of biological parents. Even if one can embrace the reality and experience of being chosen and loved, one cannot deny the reality and experience of being rejected or abandoned (unless the biological parents died or were incapable of raising their child or children). One has to process the loss or death of not knowing where one came from and why one was not with his or her original family—as most kids were.

Initially, when the Tate family took me in, and some years after, I didn't know I had been given up by someone. As far as I knew, I was in this family, and they treated me the same as any other family member. However, as I became a little older, my parents did tell me I was given up for adoption. I can't say I agonized about it or made a big deal of it. But deep down inside, I thought it was rather odd.

Another odd aspect of this situation for me was Children's Services. Not that Children's Services was a bad thing. It just seemed out of the ordinary. I thought it was strange when the Children's Services representative came to my house and asked me questions like "how do you like it here" or "are you being treated OK?" After all, no one asked my brother how he was doing. And what kind of answer would I give to a stranger who I wasn't sure was coming to aid or complicate the situation? Nevertheless, this was the only home I knew and the only place I had a family, so I always gave an affirming answer. I'm not sure when the Children's Services representative stopped coming to my house to check on me, but I know I was very young (probably between seven and ten years old) when it happened. Although the "representative" was always nice and supportive, I was glad when this "special treatment" was over so I could live as a normal member of the family. Still, as I reflect, this "adoption business" left a few more questions than answers.

Although I was never overwhelmed with my parents' admission that I was adopted or bothered by the years Children's Services visited our home, I knew something was missing. But what could it be? It certainly wasn't love, acceptance, or support. And it wasn't a desire— on my part—to be somewhere else, with somebody else. I believe it was the "why" element in relation to losing something. Lurking in the subconscious and deeper spaces of my mind, I felt a loss, a need to know what happened, and how this unique situation defined me. It seemed at an early age, I discovered that certain types of losses generate questions concerning one's world, one's identity, and one's meaning to others.

In respect to questions about my identity or place in this family, I remember when I was nine or ten years old, a so-called friend told me the truth about my family status. This so-called friend named J didn't know I already knew about being given up for adoption. But, one day, he took me aside and told me the truth. First, I was amazed that he even knew about my situation. Second, I felt like he was revealing to me that I was not an authentic member of this family. I didn't let him know it, but I was somewhat bothered by our little meeting.

Overall, my parents softened the blow of being rejected by those who brought me into this world. I had my moments of wondering "Where are they?" "Why did this happen?" And "What does this mean?" But the "unwanted" aspect of being given up for adoption never really got me down. I knew I was blessed to be a Tate. However, in recent years, I've become more curious about my history than ever before—especially because I am a father. In the 1990s, I decided to contact Children's Services to find my biological parents. After some letter-writing back and forth, I was given information leading to my birth mother. I wanted to contact my birth mother and make a connection—maybe fill in some blank space in my life, so I decided to write my birth mother a letter.

The Children's Services caseworker, who had been helping me, told me to be careful about how I talked about the adoption in case someone other than she discovered this letter. Also, she said, depending upon the situation (my birth mother feeling embarrassed or guilty, not wanting to be bothered, wanting to keep things in the past, etc.), she may not respond. So I wrote my birth mother a nice, thoughtful letter—hoping to turn an age-old loss into a gain. Here's my letter—with the exception of her name, my birthday, and the post script:

Greetings!!! I don't know if you remember me, but the first time we met was somewhere around November XX, 19XX. I've changed a lot since that time, as I know you have. The purpose in writing this letter is to let you know that I have a desire to dialogue with you. Please understand that I do not wish to intrude or interrupt your life. I will not bother you. This very letter and future communication doesn't have to involve those you're involved with. But as a husband and father, I would very much welcome an opportunity to touch base with you before I leave this earth. I pray that you would accept this sincere invitation to share with love and acceptance. Unfortunate circumstances may have kept us apart for all of these years, but it doesn't mean that we can't like each other and be friendly. We do have a bond, regardless of how that bond was established. We can't change the past, but we can do something about the present and future. Please earnestly pray and think about this request. I hope to hear from you real soon. You won't regret it!!!

Sincerely,

Jose Hardy Tate

Well, my hopes of turning a negative or loss into a positive were short-lived. I got no response. Shortly thereafter, my wife found my birth mother's telephone number on the Internet while I was overseas serving my country in the Air Force. She talked to my birth mother's husband (not my biological father) because she wouldn't talk to my wife. And, he assured my wife she had the wrong person. I was never looking to replace my adoptive parents with my biological parents because Mom and Dad will always be the only true parents I'll ever have. I thought my sincere efforts could bring about a change. I was wrong. This attempt was the last in trying to resurrect a family that had been dead to me for years.

In the Bible, Jesus resurrected Lazarus. But my aborted relationship with my biological parents would stay in the tomb. Though I acknowledge my first loss in being given up for adoption, I embrace the fact that I was chosen. I was chosen by God to be a Tate and to love and live with this family. The Lord allowed one door to close and another to open. To be sure, life wasn't always easy. Like most families, we were far from perfect, and our environment was no paradise. But I was chosen, and I gained a family. And, I learned to love and live with this family in a challenging environment.

I LOVED AND LIVED WITH THIS FAMILY IN A CHALLENGING ENVIRONMENT

Originally, my mother and father grew up in Tennessee and later moved to Ohio. My mother had three children (Chester, Billy, and Ronnie) when she married my dad in 1950. A few years later, they had my brother, Maurice. During President Kennedy's presidency, they brought me into the fold. Chester was the oldest, followed by Billy, Ronnie, Maurice, and me. Chester, Billy, and Ronnie were grown when I came along. Chester (who was mentally ill at birth) and Ronnie lived in Tennessee with my grandmother. Billy lived at another residence in town, but he would come by and stay with us every now and then. For the most part, my parents, Maurice, and I lived together.

I grew up in a low-income, low quality-of-life area. Initially, when my parents moved into the neighborhood (before I was born), it wasn't that bad. I remember when I was very young (maybe two years old), my parents, Maurice, and I lived on the second floor of an apartment-style house. When I was four years old, we moved down the street into a single-family home. But in a very short time, the neighborhood began to go down. Soon, it seemed like people were leaving the neighborhood like residents running from a burning building or rats abandoning a sinking ship—I'll have a little more to say about rats later. Of course, there were still good, decent, kind-hearted, hardworking people in our environment. But, with all the trappings and distractions around us, life was no picnic. In fact, if I had to summarize my experience of growing up in this environment, I would use the title "The Very Good, The Bad, and The Very Bad."

THE VERY GOOD...

The funny thing about living in a poor, challenging environment is, if your home life is fairly stable, you don't always realize how poor or challenged you are—at least not for some time. Even as I look back on my childhood and community, I can recall many wonderful, positive experiences.

I had good-hearted, hardworking parents who tried to give us a better life than they experienced growing up. Mom and Dad grew up in a tough environment and hostile world. They knew plenty about adversity and rejection. But they never projected that onto me. They modeled kindness, consideration, respect, and tolerance. Their actions toward others reminded me to do the same. They didn't carry chips on their shoulders or blame the world for their plight. They played the hand life dealt them. As odd as this may sound, I don't ever remember my parents being negative toward anyone or fighting between themselves— they were very good at keeping their problems hidden from others. I don't remember them as gossips or in other people's business. They kept to their own affairs. Yet they wouldn't hesitate to help someone in need. Aside from a few vices, Mom and Dad were pretty stable, and that was a good thing (a very good thing in an unstable environment).

The "very good" memories didn't stop there. Mom and Dad always gave me a nice birthday party. I'd invite my friends over, and we would play games, eat cake and ice cream, and have a good time. Along with my birthday, Christmas and Thanksgiving were my favorite times of the year. During Christmas, we would decorate a nice-sized Christmas tree, hang stockings, and put up lights. On Christmas day, we would listen to Christmas music, share gifts, laughter, and bond with each other. On Thanksgiving Day, Mom would fix a meal fit for a king, and we would eat, relax, have fun, and enjoy each other's company. And, there's more.

We had an apple tree, grapevines, and a garden in our backyard. My mother used to bake pies, make grape jelly, and cook collard greens and other vegetables from her garden. Every now and then, Mom would play fun games with me in our backyard and inside the house (cards, Monopoly, etc.). Dad and I would love to watch sports together—especially the Cleveland sports teams. We had a lot of fun cheering our teams on. However, it wasn't as much fun when the Browns, Indians, and Cavaliers lost. I almost took it personally when they would lose, which could be pretty comical as I reflect upon it.

Speaking of sports, Mom and Dad loved to see me play football. I think the love affair started when I played touch football in the streets with the other neighborhood kids. Back in the day, kids within our neighborhood would get together and play in the streets, even though we had to maneuver around parked cars and other obstacles during the course of the game. I remember one day, when I was playing with some older kids (which is normally what I did), JR sent me on a fly route and threw me this long pass that seemed too far for me to catch. Somehow, I caught up with the pass, bobbled it for a few seconds, and hauled it in for a touchdown! After the catch, I looked around, and saw Mom watching from our house. She was ecstatic that I made this play. Actually, while I was growing up, I was pretty good in all the major sports (football, basketball, and baseball), but I collected the most trophies in football. After some years of playing football in the streets and in my neighborhood, some of my friends talked to me about joining a little league football team called the East Cleveland Chiefs. If memory serves me correctly, the East Cleveland Chiefs had three teams available to join: the Termites (eight to nine years old), Peewees (ten to twelve years old), and Midgets (thirteen to fourteen years old).

Normally, age, weight, and other factors determined the group one could sign up for. I was around ten years old at the time, and playing football seem like a good idea. However, there were some expenses involved, and East Cleveland was very far from where I lived. I knew my participation in this activity would require me to sacrifice my time and effort, but Mom and Dad would have to make many sacrifices as well. I played four seasons for the Chiefs from ten to fourteen years old, and my parents supported me 100 percent.

They took me (and sometimes other kids from our neighborhood who played on the team) to practice every day. They covered expenses (equipment, travel, etc.), attended my games, and cheered me on. In 1974, my football team had an opportunity to go to Glendale, California, to play a little league team called the Bears. Part of the airfare was paid through donations, but parents had to come up with the rest. Our football team would stay with the opposing team once we got to California. To my great surprise, my parents signed us up to go, and off we went to California. That was huge! My family had never done anything like that before. It would be the first time I'd ever flown on a plane, traveled that far, and stayed with people as well off as the Bears and their families were.

While we were there, we went to places like Disneyland, the Hollywood Walk of Fame, and other neat places. And we met movie stars, such as James Garner of *The Rockford Files*. More importantly, my team (the Peewees) beat the Bears 22–0. In that game, I scored a couple of touchdowns, gained a bunch of yards catching passes, and was named the Most Valuable Player of the game. And my mom and dad were right there cheering me on. Wow, what a moment! To the casual observer, these "very good things" might not have seemed important. But when these "moments" are weighed in context with a challenging environment (just wait until we get to the "Bad" and "Very Bad"), one might understand why these special times were so significant.

As far as I can remember, Mom and Dad stressed the importance of getting an education. Dad was encouraging when he used to say, "Son, you've got to get you some book learning." This was Dad's funny way of telling me to focus on my studies. Mom was more hands-on. She would help me with my homework, go to my Parent and Teachers Association (PTA) meetings, and show great interest in my grades. An emphasis on education helped build a foundation that would serve me well in the future. Still, growing up, I achieved my best work in elementary and high school.

In the third grade, I wrote a book of poems with my peers that was published after months of hard work during the school year. Our class used the proceeds from the book to go on a trip to an amusement park. Of course, my family was delighted. Also, I appeared in a local kids' television show called *For Children Only* (a show similar to the popular kids' show called *Zoom*). In the fourth, fifth, and sixth grades, I was in enrichment classes (advanced academic level classes). I received good grades and recognition in elementary school that made my parents proud. Although my junior high school experience wasn't quite as sterling, I seemed to soar again in high school.

In the tenth grade, I was a member of our chess club and later designated as the captain, and I made good grades. In the eleventh grade, I received the Martha Holden Jennings Award and $500 toward my college education for demonstrating improvement from the previous year, played junior varsity football (our team went undefeated), and was a writer and contributor to our high school newspaper, the *Blue and Gold*. My grades continued to soar. In the twelfth grade, I was the sports editor of the *Blue and Gold*. I had a column on the sports page called "Tate's Talk," where I discussed current sports events. I was a staff member and contributor for our yearbook, played varsity football and received a letter and trophy after the season (having a letter on your school sweater was pretty cool in those days), and was second runner-up for homecoming king. I won a scholarship from the *Cleveland Press* newspaper (no longer in service) for writing, and made the honor roll several times. I was even voted "Best Personality" in my 1979 yearbook (along with a female senior).

My parents were right there to cheer me on from elementary to high school. It was great to have them at all of life's important events. Unfortunately, this would soon change—a change that would affect the rest of my life. But, for now, I want to concentrate on the "very good" aspects of loving and living with my family in a challenging environment. I've talked about family, love and support, sports, and education. But my early embracing of God, church, and faith would set me on a course—though the course would have many twists and turns—that would impact my life to this very day.

My mother and grandmother had an early influence on my spirituality and faith. My grandmother became a Christian at an early age and later raised my mother and aunt in a local Baptist church in Knoxville, Tennessee. My mother continued her faith and membership in the Baptist community and would later introduce me to the Christian faith. When I was a child, my mother took me to her Baptist church and allowed me to attend a Methodist church closer to home—actually just around the corner. Between visiting my devout grandmother in the summers, observing Christian virtues in my mother, and attending church (and Sunday school), my religious foundation was beginning to form. However, when I was eleven years old, I had a unique experience with the Lord.

Around June 1973, my mother and I traveled to Knoxville, Tennessee, to spend a month or so with my grandmother and other relatives. During my visit, my adult brother (Ronnie) took his stepson (AR) and me to a baseball game. During the game, my brother and I got into an argument. After the game, my brother and I began to argue again. While in the parking lot, my brother threatened to chastise me for misbehaving and being disrespectful. I told him he would not touch me. Then I ran away from him. I kept running and running and running until I didn't know where I was. I was lost, afraid, and in potential danger traveling down unfamiliar streets through the city. Out of nowhere, something welled up in me, and I began to talk to God. Although I'd never done this before, I lifted my voice to heaven and asked God to please help me find my way back home.

After what seemed to be several hours later, God did it! The Lord miraculously led me back home (to my grandmother's house), unharmed, and into the arms of my family. Needless to say, my family was not very pleased with my actions. They had spent most of the day worrying and searching for me, but they were more than glad when I made it safely home. Later that year, I accepted the Lord and was baptized. It was a watershed moment. Not a moment that transformed me into a spiritual giant, but a moment that would catapult me on the journey of my life. Spiritual growth is an ongoing process that often takes a lifetime. I'm just grateful God showed me at an early age how lost I would be without him. I didn't really grasp all the significant insights from that experience overnight. But, throughout my life, God would let me know he was with me, even when others weren't or couldn't be there. Several years ago, my nephew reminded me of that incident. His words were something like, "Man, I still don't know how you made it back from the stadium." We both laughed.

I find it very encouraging to look back and acknowledge the "very good" aspects of my early life. This type of reflection is a reminder that few situations are totally bad or undesirable. And, if I look at my life long enough, I can always find something positive to be thankful for. However, as I balance the reality of my upbringing, I must acknowledge the undesirable side of life. Since we all live in an imperfect, fallible, challenging world, I'm sure most people can identify with hardship, pain, suffering, and loss. Still, everyone's story is different. Here's where my story of the "very good" aspects of my early life with my family ends, and the "bad" and the "very bad" realities of those days began.

THE BAD...

I remember several years ago when I was a young enlisted man in the Air Force, I had a conversation with another airman about our backgrounds. During our conversation, I asked the airman, "What kind of background do you think I came from?" The airman smiled with confidence and said, "Oh, you grew up in the suburbs." In the airman's mind, she was paying me a compliment because I appeared to come from a solid background and a stable environment, free from the distractions and negativity found in less desirable places. In addition, this airman didn't see any wounds from an individual rejected at birth or an individual raised with real challenges inside and outside the home. The airman didn't see any scars or baggage. And I didn't display a certain language, attitude, or behavior that would alert people that I had come from the wrong side of the tracks. In her mind, I was young, hardworking, smart, likable, and well mannered with a bright future ahead. When I told her where I was from and some of my story, she was shocked! She was shocked because I wasn't supposed to be the person I appeared to be coming from the type of environment where I was raised. We continued to share, appreciate each other's stories, and move on from there. Yet I still think about that moment, and what it meant to grow up and experience the "bad" in my environment—to deal with dysfunction and negativity inside and outside the home. In reflection, here's what it looked like, how it felt, and how it challenged us.

I grew up seeing my neighborhood go from nice houses, clean streets, and thriving businesses to run-down homes, vacant lots, beaten-up empty buildings, nasty streets, and fleeing businesses. I saw good friends and families leave the neighborhood, and I wondered why our family didn't leave too. But Mom and Dad weren't the kind of people who did a lot of moving around. Plus, I think they got used to calling our environment home and held out hope that things would get better. Yet inside, they must have known it would only get worse.

Soon, I would live in a climate where crime, drug and alcohol abuse, promiscuous sex, gang activity, violence, and an attitude of apathy and tension pervaded our environment. I don't believe having limited resources, living in poverty, and having few advantages automatically make people not care about themselves, their environment, or one another; however, I must admit, living in these types of conditions doesn't do much for the psyche or the soul. Living in this type of environment is like trying to climb a mountain in a forty-pound gorilla suit with a backpack full of bricks. It may not be impossible to climb that mountain, but it seems to take everything you've got! Although this is an overview of the external pressures my family and I faced, we had plenty of internal challenges within our home as well. On this note, let me get more specific and personal in sharing some situations that bring the "bad" a little closer to home.

I saw drugs and alcohol abuse ruin many people's lives. When this scenario touches one's home, the pain is almost too much to bear. My brother, Billy, was the second oldest among the siblings. He worked downtown and had two children. In his younger days, Billy was a handsome, strong, athletic man who looked like he should be playing for the Cleveland Browns. He was witty, practical, and down-to-earth. He loved jazz and had a quick mind. Billy was a man's man whose stature and presence caused those around him to take notice. My brother could have been a leader of men because I could see that potential in his life. In fact, he could have been anything he wanted to be. However, Billy had quite a temper (his nickname was "scrap iron") and was hurting on the inside—soured by the ills of society and the storms of life. He often took refuge in the bottle. But I've never known the contents within a bottle to change anyone's circumstances or make one's problems go away. If anything, it magnifies the problems and makes a person's attitude, outlook, and coping skills even worse.

Maurice, my other brother, had a good heart and was mainly interested in having a good time. Maurice eventually worked downtown with Billy and never had any children. Maurice had an infectious laugh, was friendly to most he came in contact with, and had lots of talent. Maurice played the drums, guitar, and listened to all types of music—

although I think his preference was hard rock. My brother's love for different kinds of music influenced my early appreciation for all types of music. Growing up, I'd listen to rock and roll, folk music, pop music, soul music, rhythm and blues, and disco. Listening to different types of music allowed me to appreciate how people from different places in life expressed themselves.

However, Maurice was too influenced by the culture and times. When the Woodstock train left the station in the 1960s, some in the neighborhood got on board. However, not only did Maurice get on board, he never got off! The 1960s and Woodstock didn't invent the idea of experimenting with drugs, engaging in casual sex, or being suspicious of the government, parents, or anyone over forty years old. But this era sure did lend a little gasoline to the flame. And my brother fully bought into some of these ideas. In addition, my beloved brother wasn't very ambitious or overly concerned about employment. He liked to hang out and be among the people—sometimes, the wrong type of people. He was a people pleaser who wanted to fit into the crowd and was easily influenced by others. His so-called buddies partied with him and watched him sink in a sea of indulges. Yet they never seemed to sink as low as he did. In reality, I can't blame the culture, the environment, or his friends for my brother's life choices. Each man or woman (especially upon adulthood) is responsible for his or her own choices. Yet I can't help but feel our environment was like living in a minefield—too many vices within one's reach that can damage mind, body, and soul.

Ronnie was the third oldest who grew up in Tennessee. He served a few years in the military, got out, and moved back home. He had more children than my other brothers, and his wife was a nice sister-in-law. Ronnie used to come up and visit us when he could, and I always liked seeing my big brother. We had our little scrapes (like when I ran from him at the stadium after a ball game), but we loved each other. Ronnie was personable, engaging, witty, and knowledgeable. I remember when I visited him, it seemed like he knew everybody. He used to joke and say, "This is my town," and I'd just smile, thinking, *He's pretty cool.*

Ronnie liked to play chess, checkers, and cards. Sometimes, my brother and I would play chess for hours. In his younger days, Ronnie was no stranger to the ladies, and he possessed a certain charm. Also, he had a business mind and was good with numbers—too good. Ronnie had the skills and talent to do great things; but the street life was too alluring, and it pulled him in. Eventually, poor choices would cost him years of his life—years you can't get back. Like me, he lived in a minefield. In the end, the key to living in a minefield is to be extra careful where you step or how you live in order to survive the environment.

Drug and alcohol abuse, the street life, and less desirable role models weren't the only negative realities that influenced members within our family; there were other challenges as well. Up to this point, I've spoken highly of my parents because they were wonderful people. But, for a moment, I'll take off the rose-colored glasses and reveal some less admirable qualities. I know that living in a very stressful, challenging, and dangerous situation took years off their lives because Mom worried too much and Dad kept too much inside. As they got older, Mom dealt with heart problems, high blood pressure, and some anxiety. Dad went a little further into the cave—not becoming involved in the community or establishing more meaningful relationships with family and friends. In addition to stress, they didn't maintain the healthiest lifestyle. A below-average diet and poor eating habits, lack of exercise, and smoking put their bodies at risk. Medically, it's a proven fact that if we don't take care of our bodies, we will eventually suffer. My parents didn't do the best job of taking care of their temples, and their temples suffered. All these things withstanding, the most controversial side of my parents would be how they spoiled us.

I never got around to asking my parents why they didn't get after us more than they did. I surmise it was from wanting to do more for us (Maurice and me) than what was done for them and not wanting to intimidate us or impose their will on us. Don't get me wrong—I didn't totally escape being disciplined or punished. But my parents were more laid back and easy on us than they needed to be. Furthermore, Mom and Dad were not particularly demanding of us when it came to doing chores and being on our best behavior at home and in the neighborhood. A number of incidents come to mind.

My brother and I didn't have a lot of chores as some of our friends did. Sure, from time to time, we shoveled the snow in the winter and picked up apples and leaves in the yard in the summer and fall. But my parents did more than their share around our house. My parents did not use chores, assigned tasks, or duties as the main source in challenging or grooming us to become responsible, self-sufficient people for the future. They provided a supportive home and trusted that we would develop and refine those conscientious, responsible, independence-producing skills outside the home. My participation in school, sports, and church did help me grow, but Maurice did not fare as well. Overall, we would have matured more and been better equipped emotionally had my parents been more conscientious in mentoring and training us for the outside world. If the positive side of spoiling one's children is giving them a sense of feeling special and not imposing one's will on them, the negative side is allowing them to develop mindsets or behaviors that are not in their best interests. Let me further explain by offering a few more examples.

Although boys will be boys, boys need much guidance and grooming to become men. When I was a young boy, I liked the girls, and the girls seemed to like me. However, on a couple of occasions, my being a "fresh" boy rubbed some parents the wrong way. The first incident happened when I was no more than six or eight years old. I was over at a neighbor's house playing doctor in the backyard with his daughters and other kids, when the father—Mr. W—came out from the house into the yard and caught us red-handed. I gathered myself together and ran home—actually a couple of houses down from his house. Mr. W followed me to my house and promptly told my parents about my shenanigans. But my parents said very little to me about it, and I don't remember getting into any trouble.

A few years later a similar incident happened, only this time, a neighbor summoned my mother from her house to tell her that I was running around and chasing my female friends. Mom heard her, but she didn't demand that I behave or stop fooling around. In fact, years later this same neighbor told me how frustrated she was with my mom because she felt Mom blew her off and didn't take the situation more seriously. I'm sure Mom didn't mean to hurt her feelings; she probably felt that boys will be boys, and I'd grow out of it. Plus, I was a momma's boy, and momma believed her son was a good boy.

Actually, I was a good boy, but my gravitation toward the opposite sex needed to be checked. No greater example of this was the activity that took place at my birthday parties. I don't know when it started, but we had this ritual of playing "spin the bottle" at my birthday parties. To play "spin the bottle," everyone gets in a circle, a bottle is put in the middle of the group, someone spins the bottle, and whomever the bottle points to can kiss anyone of the opposite sex in the group. We would play "spin the bottle" with my parents in the house in full view. I don't recall ever being reproved or corrected for this. Perhaps my parents figured we were too young and innocent to be really affected by kissing one another. Today, we all know better. Yet there's more.

I remember going in my brother's room—against my mother's wishes, even though she must have known I didn't stop—on countless occasions and seeing pictures and magazines not suitable for my young eyes to see. As the years went on and I became older, my brother's room became a less desirable or virtuous place for a teenager to visit. My parents knew my brother's appetite had become very self-serving and debilitating, but they did little about it. During my teenage years, my desire to engage in some "hanky-panky" started to grow, but my parents did little to redirect my "youthful passions."

Fortunately, the fleshly fires within did not totally consume me. Nevertheless, this does not mean I didn't engage in activity that would have served me best in a more sacred relationship, such as marriage. Someone once said, "Everything good to you isn't good for you." Today, I have only one child who can legitimately call me dad. Considering my past, this is nothing short of a miracle. In retrospect, I don't believe my parents realized the impact their passivity or spoiling would have on my brothers and me. They grew up in hard times when parents could be very harsh in how they disciplined and corrected their children. I'm sure growing up with very strict parents in a difficult environment played a major role in how they raised us—not wanting to inflict the same pain on us they had experienced.

Back in their day—and even when I was growing up—it was common for parents to grab a switch, stick, belt, cord, or anything they could get their hands on, and beat the heck out of their children. It was not uncommon for parents to smack their children "into next week" for unacceptable behavior. Although, my parents were far from people who regularly used harsh discipline to keep us in line, I do recall a couple of occasions when my dad must have had a flashback or two. The first situation happened when I was around five or six years old. My mother said something to me while we were both in the kitchen, and as I walked away and left the kitchen, I began to say things under my breath. I didn't know my dad was watching me jerk, twist, and act defiant. As I was clowning in the next room, my dad comes out of nowhere and whips me with his newspaper—the funny papers were no longer funny.

Another incident happened when I was around seven or eight years old when my dad thought I did something I didn't do. Dad thought I took something that was his (and he probably had a good reason to think this way); but, on this occasion, I hadn't done it. So Dad asked the question, "What happened?" When I didn't give him the answer he was looking for—*bam*—there I went! He knocked me to the floor, and I saw stars—and I'm not talking about famous celebrities. I ran crying to my room, surprised and shaken by my dad's wrath, which I rarely saw or experienced. Fortunately, Dad showed me some love a little later. Although, as a parent, I would not advocate striking one's child in such a manner, parents need to discipline their children and set healthy boundaries for them. Since my dad only knocked me down once and rarely physically punished me, I can truthfully say I probably deserved to have my coattail pulled a little more because it's better to get the proper discipline in the home as opposed to getting it outside the home—where undesirable behavior can cause a person a world of trouble.

The last point I'll mention regarding the few areas my parents lacked is "hammering home" information. Again, I'll be the first to say, being a parent isn't easy, and telling someone something over and over again can be very exhausting. But I think Mom and Dad articulated sage wisdom to us more in passing than repetitively doing so. We didn't get many teaching moments about sex, relationships, or how to make it in this crazy world. Perhaps they experienced or witnessed parents struggling to lead and guide rebellious kids or teenagers—raising my brothers and me was no picnic. Or, as I previously mentioned, maybe they thought we'd figure it out along the way. Whatever the case, I don't blame my parents. No parent is perfect (neither am I), and we all have our flaws and deficiencies. I do know they loved us very much and would not intentionally do anything that would cause us problems later in life. Overall, I recognize the "Bad" as a part of my history, but I've learned my history doesn't have to define my present and future. Through it all, I continued to love and appreciate my family and our journey during the very good and bad times. And, when times became even harder, I still considered myself grateful to be in this family. In light of this, I must recall the "Very Bad" aspects of the past.

THE VERY BAD...

When I was growing up, if someone said, "Man that suit was bad," the person could actually be giving someone a compliment because *bad* sometimes meant *good*. However, if someone said, "Man that suit was very bad" usually the person actually meant what he or she was saying— the suit was very bad or awful! There's no confusion or misinterpretation about something that's "very bad." When a person uses the term "very bad," he or she means to articulate a powerful message to the receiver(s) that the assessment of the given subject supersedes any concept or idea of what would normally be considered "bad." In the same vein, when I speak about certain aspects of my environment, I must make others aware that the term "bad" is insufficient and lacks the depths to describe this experience. Upon reflection, my family and I were often interrupted by the "very bad" realities of life. Living in a minefield can produce "very bad" results. In categorizing some of the land mines my family or I experienced (directly or indirectly) during my preteen and teenage years, I would define them in five categories: Poverty, Assault, Abuse, Murder, and Tragedy.

Although there are different levels of poverty, my experience of growing up around poverty is consistent with having few resources, limited funds, limited access to quality health care, high crime, violence, promiscuity, welfare, substance abuse, low-quality schools, and living in a poor environment. I will speak to some of these aspects of poverty later. For now, I want to focus on my experience in living in a poor environment.

Similar to what I said earlier, I remember houses going from decent to dilapidated; nice apartment buildings going to abandon buildings; property where houses, buildings, and stores once stood proudly going to empty, dirty lots; cars going from functional to junk left to rot in fields or in someone's backyard; and big dead rats in the street as I walked to school (the stench from the rats was sickening). Speaking of rats (and mice), I saw plenty of them up close and personal in my home.

Once, when I was playing on the floor with my toys, a rat ran across the floor. One of my favorite childhood entertainers, the late Michael Jackson, may have once considered these jokers friends, but, trust me— they were no friend of mine! After my heart jumped back in my chest, I ran for my dad to kill the rat. At the time, Dad was a sanitation engineer (as I used to say), so he wasn't afraid of them. In fact, Dad was called on quite a bit to rescue me in these "emergency" situations. Another time, my father, mother, and I were watching television when

I noticed something moving on one of our curtains near the piano. To my surprise, a mouse was climbing on the curtain—perhaps bored with remaining anonymous between the furniture on the floor. Of course, I yelled, "Dad, there's a mouse on the curtain!" Needless to say, the mouse's days where numbered. There were other times I dealt with rats or mice under my bed or other places in my room, in the kitchen, basement, or outside near our garbage cans. Whenever and wherever I ran across them, it was an unhappy, ugly moment. By the way, the roaches were not fun either (although I'd choose them over Mickey Mouse and his relatives any day of the week).

As uninviting as living in a poor environment can be, I didn't realize how poor I was until I went to California to play football with the East Cleveland Chiefs. Before my trip, I knew we didn't have a lot of money or great clothes or wonderful living conditions or the safest, cleanest environment. But, at twelve years old when I got back from California (after staying with my suburban, rival football team), I knew something was terribly wrong. I discovered everyone wasn't living in the conditions I lived in. When I returned home, it took some time for me to get back into the rhythm of living in my environment. However, I don't think I was ever the same. I remember asking my parents if we could move to a better environment—perhaps something in the range of my rival team in California. But, we never got around to leaving this area. So my longing to rid myself of poverty continued. Yet the "very bad" realities didn't stop there. Assault, Abuse, Murder, and Tragedy were next.

An assault is very traumatic and injurious to the physical, mental, and spiritual well-being of an individual. Assaults can leave one with emotional scars long after the physical injuries are gone. In reflection, I'm sure the assault my loved ones and I experienced during my upbringing impacted my life. Fortunately, God allowed me to work through these painful memories and use them to strengthen my character. This notwithstanding, here are a few incidents that come to mind.

At the time of this unfortunate incident, I was around eight years old. I just started riding a fairly new bicycle when I decided to go bike riding with my friends. On this particular day, four or five of my friends and I rode our bikes a good distance from our neighborhood. Although I wasn't totally sure how far we were going or how long we would be, I felt pretty comfortable because my friends were a little older than I—plus we were in a group. We rode together as a group; but once we approached this steep hill, I got behind them. One by one, each of my friends rode his bike down this hill. As each person rode his bike down the hill, we all laughed a little because each person looked funny trying to keep control of his bike (and his composure) as the bike's speed increased riding down this hill.

Now, it was my turn. I was the last person left to feel the excitement and thrill of going down this hill. So I gathered myself, and slowly began to go down the hill. Suddenly out of nowhere, a boy ran up from behind me, hit me in the head with a chain, knocked me off my bike, and stole my bicycle. For a few moments (which seemed like eternity), I lay on the ground in shock, disbelief, and pain as I watched this boy take my bike and dash off in the opposite direction. Once I came to my senses, I cried out to my friends with a loud voice that this boy had stolen my bike. They doubled back and tried to catch the thief, but he was too fast for them to catch. I think we all were amazed this event happened because I wasn't that far behind my friends. My friends probably thought I was right behind them when they got down the hill, and no one stopped to make sure we were still all together.

After this incident, we gathered ourselves and rode our bikes back home. I rode with one of my friends on his bike. However, this incident left me shaken and humiliated. When I got home, I cried and told my parents what happened. I'm sure they comforted me. I know they must have encouraged me and told me I would get another bike. But I don't remember what they said. All I know is someone knocked me in my head and took something valuable from me. He didn't know or care anything about my family, my life, or me. He didn't care how this incident might affect my mind or sense of security. No, as a bully preys on the weak and vulnerable, this boy selfishly imposed his will upon me and took advantage of the situation. Fortunately, this demoralizing assault didn't break me. But a few other "very bad" moments would test my soul.

I was seven or eight years old in grade school when this terrible event took place. Mr. RL was my teacher, and we had between twenty and thirty children in class. One day as the students were participating in class, a bee entered the room. As the bee flew throughout the room, kids got excited and began to duck, dodge, and make noise. Perhaps, I was a bit more animated because wasps had stung me while visiting my grandmother during the summer—and I knew that experience was no fun. As the bee came my way, I remember raising my voice and moving out of the way for cover. Suddenly, out of nowhere, Mr. RL singled me out, kicked me in the behind, and angrily admonished me. The room became quiet—only a few whispered. Some of the kids who had been moving or afraid of being stung by the bee were now more afraid of Mr. RL.

I felt humiliated, embarrassed, and angry. I remember crying until my eyes were red, hyperventilating, shaking, and feeling powerless. Although Mr. RL never displayed this type of reckless behavior before and was generally a decent guy, he lost his composure that day. As a class, we had been writing poems to incorporate into a book of poems as a fundraiser to go on a trip to an amusement park at the end of the school year. I had some of the best poems in the class, but after he kicked me, I tore my poems apart.

About fifteen to twenty minutes after the incident, Mr. RL realized he had gone too far. He came to me and apologized. I'm sure he meant it; but I was still reeling from this event. Also, he took my poems and tried to piece them back together. After school, I remember going home and telling my parents what happened. For the most part, my parents were not the kind of people who would go ballistic on a teacher for inappropriately punishing their child, so I don't know what they did in terms of contacting the school or Mr. RL. I do know that we didn't talk much about the incident after I told them what happened.

Mr. RL apologized again and tried to make amends. We did salvage my poems, and I was a major contributor to our class book of poems—and we did have fun at the amusement park at the end of the year. As a child, I didn't dwell on the assault or carry bitter feelings toward Mr. RL. I survived the experience and kept moving on. At least, I thought I did. In reflection, I think I tucked away this event, like other painful events in my life. But painful events can stay tucked away for only so long. I didn't realize until much, much later in life that the "very bad" moments of the past had scarred me to the point that I struggled (as an adult) with being defensive, quick-tempered, or upset toward those whom I felt wanted to slight, hurt, bully, or intimidate me. However, I thank God for making a tremendous difference in this area of my life because, if it weren't for Him, I would have been consumed with anger and bitterness. Still, some painful events take much time to overcome. And coping with the fact that someone in your family has been victimized can be very challenging to overcome as well.

In my life, I've discovered that a mother-and-son relationship is a very special one. Although my adoptive mother did not give birth to me, our bond was very strong. I was my mother's son, and I was very protective of her. Someone could argue that being protective of my mother was unnecessary because most people who knew her loved, cared for, and respected her. And, most would describe her as a person "who wouldn't hurt a fly." Unfortunately, a despicable individual failed to take my mother's humanity and character into consideration and did the unthinkable to my sweet mother.

One day my mother got off from work and took three or four buses to our neighborhood, as she normally did. After my mother got off the bus, she had to walk quite a distance to our home. When she reached our street, some hideous person jumped out of nowhere, grabbed my mother, slung her to the ground, and grabbed her purse. After the assault, my mother walked home. When she came home, her arms were bloodied and bruised, her clothes were dirty and torn, and she was devastated—although she tried not to act like she was. Let me pause right here and say, I lived in an environment where if someone even talked about your mother, those were fighting words. If someone just made the statement, "Your mama," he didn't have to finish the sentence because he knew "it was on."

So here stands before me, my precious mother, bloodied, banged up, and treated like some animal! I couldn't have been more than eleven or twelve years old, but I left home, got some friends, and went looking for this abuser. I'm not sure how much damage we could or would have done, but I was very angry. Fortunately, we never caught the perpetrator. Of course, I didn't feel that way at the time. As I look back on the situation, I know that God was watching over me! I'm glad we didn't catch the perpetrator because my actions could have changed the course of my life. I could have made the biggest mistake of my life by taking matters into my own hands. Still, I felt powerless and violated because my mom was violated and victimized.

It would take some time for my mother to heal from this event, and I'm sure it took even more time for my mother to get beyond this event emotionally. Mom was a worrier, with high blood pressure and other medical concerns. So this act did not help the situation. But we dealt with it the best we could, and we continued to stay in the neighborhood. Ah yes, the good old neighborhood filled with land mines, booby traps, and quicksand. Sometimes, living in the neighborhood felt like "crabs living in a bucket." As soon a one crab tries to move forward or get to the top, another crab tries to bring him back to the bottom of the bucket. However, no matter how difficult the challenge, my parents wanted us to keep moving forward. And we did. Yet those challenging, painful situations continued.

As I mentioned earlier, my brother Maurice was a people pleaser and one who had a knack for aligning himself with people who didn't have his best interests at heart. I don't remember the year, but I do remember it was warm outside when Maurice's life almost came to an end. He was around seventeen or eighteen years old on that fateful night, and I was ten or eleven years old. I can't remember whether someone came to the house or called, but we were notified my brother had been walking down the street when someone shot him in his neck.

I remember my father leaving the house and going to the hospital to be with my brother. My mother tried to stay calm but was visibly upset. I remember feeling afraid, sad, and powerless (again). All I could do was wait and hope my brother would pull through. Thank God, he did. And, when he finally came home, he verified the story told to my parents. In fact, we were told the bullet was inches away from killing him. Of course, my parents and I were mortified by the whole ordeal. Questions about this situation seemed to fill the air, but I don't remember a lot of discussion about it. For the time being, my brother's confession about his near death experience was accepted.

However, years later I was told the truth. LR (my brother's so-called friend) told me Maurice was not walking down the street when he was shot; he was shot in PW's basement. Apparently, LR, PW , Maurice, and others were fooling around with a gun when it discharged, and my brother was shot. After the shooting, these so-called friends panicked and deliberated putting my brother in a big canister and dumping him in the river. Instead, they decided to lie about what happened, and it worked. Needless to say, LR lost a lot of credibility in my mind in terms of being a friend to my brother. Unfortunately, I believe he would later prove to be an even greater betrayer of my brother than we could ever know.

The next challenging issues in my environment were sex and spouse/significant other abuse. Although it could be argued some people experienced different types of abuse in my neighborhood, such as drug and alcohol abuse, mental and emotional abuse, and physical abuse (excessive beatings), I recall a few cases involving sex and spousal abuse that saddened my heart.

First, let me say, I narrowly escaped being a victim of child sexual abuse at a very early age. There was a boy (NW) who was probably fifteen or sixteen years old (when I was about seven or eight years old) who was very friendly. NW was kind, accepting, and seemed to take a liking to me. One day, NW invited me to his home. I accepted his invitation. No one was there but us. NW began talking and acting overly nice. Soon, NW began discussing touching me, and he started to get closer to me. In those days, I was pretty quick and slippery. When NW came toward me, I ran past him out his house and hurried home.

I was scared nearly to death. My heart was racing, and I felt weird — considering he wanted to touch and do things to me that a much older male would do with a female. I was confused as to why he wanted to do that to me. Surely, I did nothing to cause these feelings in him to occur. Yet there I was, running from a child molester. I told my parents about it, but I don't remember what they said or did. After this, I didn't see NW much. On one or two occasions when he saw me, he tried to pretend the incident never happened. From that time on, I learned to watch out for these types of individuals. Thank God this individual never bothered me again. Unfortunately, I had a few friends in the neighborhood who were not as fortunate as I.

S and T were sisters between fourteen and sixteen years old during the time they were in the neighborhood (several years older than I was). I remember them as very kind and friendly toward me. Also, they were pretty girls who looked a little older than their age. In a very short period of time, it seemed like S and T went from ordinary fun-loving girls to troubled teenagers. At first, I couldn't understand why my friends seemed to change; later, I learned that their mother's boyfriend was sexually abusing them.

Most people on my street knew the mother's boyfriend, and when the word got out, people didn't like him very much. Still, one could see how this man's sick behavior affected those girls. S's and T's countenances and attitudes changed. I believe it changed how they felt about themselves, their bodies, and life. An evil man took S's and T's innocence away, and his actions set them on a course of destruction.

Once the word got out, I didn't see S and T much anymore. They moved away from the neighborhood; and every now and then, I would hear something about them from one of our neighbors. I was shocked and saddened these things happened to my friends, and I missed them. From time to time, I've wondered how they made it as adults, and whether they ever overcame these events. I pray that they did.

My father never laid a hand on my mother (at least to my knowledge), so I was shocked and dismayed at the abuse my friends' relatives endured. LW , D, and D's family were friends of mine. Actually, LW was a relative from out of town, who stayed with the family for a while, and D lived across the street in the projects with his family. LW was around my age (fourteen or fifteen) and D was probably four or five years younger than we were but was very stout for his age. I had a very good relationship with this family, and later I would date LW's cousin for several years. Usually, our meeting place was at D's house since they lived across the street. I remember D's mother as a very sweet and kind woman. She treated me like one of her own, and I don't recall her ever being rude or disrespectful to anyone. However, I believe D's father watched too many "Super Fly" or "The Mack" movies because he thought he was "mister cool."

D's father was tall, well built, and trash talked. In fact, he once joked about doing harm to my family—at least I believe he was joking. When D's father drank and smoked weed, it negatively influenced his already over-the-top personality. His personality notwithstanding, D's father treated me well and never hurt me. So I never hesitated in going around any of LW's or D's family members. Things soon would change. I remember going over to D's house, and his mother had a black eye, and she didn't look well. Things got worse, to the point that D's mother left the home. Then D's father began losing control of his life. The abuse and dysfunction took its toll on this family.

I know it was hard on D, his older sister, and mother because I could see the hurt, pain, and anger in their faces. Soon LW left town, and D's family moved to another location. Although I would hear bits and pieces about this family, I didn't see LW or D after that. I hope the rest of their lives were smoother than what they experienced growing up. I can't even imagine how I would have turned out if my father had beaten my mother. The fact that my close friends went through this experience was damaging enough. Living in an environment filled with poverty, assaults, and abuse is hard enough; but dealing with murders and tragedies is even harder.

During my childhood, there were several murders that took place, but a couple stand out in my memory. I didn't know AW very well, but his brother, MW , and I were good friends. MW was a few years older than I (if I was eight years old, he probably was twelve). He came from a big family, and some of his family members were known throughout the neighborhood for being tough. To some extent, MW had family members who participated in gang activity. During the time MW and I were friends, he was fairly young and had not moved in the direction of some of his brothers. However, at the time, being a friend of MW had its perks. Because of our relationship, few people bothered me. In fact, I remember an incident that happened on my porch one day.

JR and I were sitting on my porch eating sandwiches when some of the W gang were walking down our street. I didn't see them coming toward us because I went in the house to get something and left JR (who was probably eleven or twelve years old) on my porch eating his sandwich. When I returned to JR, he was wiping the sandwich off his face. While I was away, the W gang bullied JR, took his sandwich, and mashed it in his face. After these guys left, JR said he wanted to get a gun and get those guys. Fortunately, JR's anger subsided, and he never sought revenge. As I thought about the incident, the W gang could have easily waited until I came back out of the house, but I knew they didn't because of my friendship with MW. However, I think they wanted to flex their muscles and show why they needed to be feared—and most people in the neighborhood did fear them. However, flexing one's muscles and striking fear in the hearts of others has its repercussions—one day, someone killed MW's brother (AW).

AW was a few years older than MW. I wasn't around him much and didn't know him very well. From afar, AW didn't seem like a bad kid. But MW's family had a negative reputation, and it seems AW got caught up in that and was killed. I was told he was murdered execution style. How terrible for a young life to be snuffed out! I wish I could say this was a random incident that happened only on occasion in my neighborhood but, sadly, it wasn't. I could name more individuals from the neighborhood who were murdered, but I'll just name one more. N's murder was a blow because I knew and liked him very much.

N was the storeowner of my favorite store up the street from my house. I'm not sure how long N's store had been there, but it was a popular fixture in my neighborhood well into my teens. I'm not sure how old N was, but if I had to guess, I'd say he was in his late thirties or early forties before his death. N was a tall, long-faced man who looked serious but was a nice guy. Sometimes people would come in the store and try to give N a hard time, but he never seemed to take it personally. Often, he could be playful in admonishing "fresh" kids by getting his little stick and driving them out his store. Yet we all knew N wouldn't hurt anyone. On a couple of occasions I saw kids stealing pops, ice creams, or bags of chips from the store; and when N caught them, he would correct or admonish them. Eventually, he would welcome them back in his store.

One day I got a foolish idea in my head to take an ice cream sandwich from his ice cream box and leave the store. I went in the store, looked around and thought I saw N busy with other customers. I took the ice cream, and slid out of the door. However, as I left the store, out of the corner of my eye, I felt N watching me. I just knew N would say something to me (or my parents) the next time I came into the store. However, the next time I went back to N's store for something, N did not say a word to me about the incident. Instead, he gave me a look that said, *I know what you did, but you're better than that.* I never stole from him or anybody else again.

One day I went to the store, and N wasn't there. This was odd because N seemed to always be there. So I asked around and was told N was murdered execution style in the back of his store. AW, now N. I couldn't believe it. Not N! He was a good guy, a fixture in the neighborhood, a caring man, and someone I looked up to. Now he was gone. I was very young at the time, but my environment was causing me to grow up fast! Kids shouldn't have to deal with the traumatic issues I've talked about, but I guess that's part of living in a field full of land mines. I wish the land mines had ceased after the poverty, assaults, abuses, and murders. But it didn't. Tragedies seemed to be a part of the landscape as well. Not that N and other situations I mentioned could not fall in a tragic category, but I recall a few situations during my pre-adult years that were untimely and deadly. And, although I'm sure we weren't the only ones to suffer such events, these tragedies made living in my environment less livable.

During my growing up years (well into my teens), kids loved to play in the streets. We would play football, kickball, baseball, and other games. As I mentioned earlier, we would play around parked cars, run in people's yards, and have a good time. Of course, the danger of playing in the street is running into a parked car, landing hard on the sidewalk, or getting hit by a car coming down the street. One day, I was playing in the street with my friends, having a good time, when I decided to go back to my house. Seconds after I got into my house, I heard this loud "boom" sound. Then I heard people screaming and crying. Immediately, I left the house and started walking down the street, but my parents called me back home. Before I turned around to go back home, I could see a car had hit someone. Later, I would learn it was DD.

I remember DD being a four-year-old kid who came from a dysfunctional family—his mom and dad fought a lot. On this particular day, a car was coming down the street. I'm not sure if he jumped in front of the car or whether the driver wasn't paying attention or going too fast, but he hit DD. Nevertheless, people on our street were devastated. I wasn't much older than DD, so I didn't know what to make of his untimely, tragic death. One minute I was playing in the street with him, and the next minute he was gone. Furthermore, if I had not gone home, I could have been hit as well. I asked my parents if I could go to his funeral, and they said I could. DD's funeral was the first I had ever attended. I remember going up to DD's casket and seeing someone in the casket who didn't seem like the kid I knew. All these years later, I can still see DD in that casket. I'm not sure what happened to the driver who killed him, but DD's parents didn't stay in the neighborhood much longer after that. This tragedy broke them down. In fact, I believe they divorced. DD's tragedy took away some of my innocence, and his death let me know how fragile life could be. I wish I could say DD's tragedy was the only sad event that touched my life. Years later, there would be another.

The year was 1973. I remember it so well because this tragic event indirectly led to another painful event. JW was a good friend of mine who lived around the block from me. JW had an older brother around nineteen years old, an older sister around fifteen or sixteen years old, and a younger sister around eight or nine years old. JW lived in the projects with his mother and siblings, minus his older brother, who occasionally came to the house but stayed somewhere else. JW and his siblings had different fathers, and his mother was attractive and looked very young (almost too young to have a nineteen-year-old). I never met JW's father, and I believe his family was on welfare at the time. JW and I hung out a lot together. We would play, eat, and spend the night at each other's house. I don't believe our parents ever met one another, and none of his siblings ever came over to my house, but I got along well with his family, and he got along with mine. Since JW's brother, EW , was considerably older than we were, he wasn't around us much. When EW was around, he didn't say much, but he was friendly. I remember him being tall, slender, athletic, and having a big Afro. Also, the ladies were attracted to EW—which hardly went unnoticed in my environment.

From what I could tell, JW's mother was pretty close to EW and had high hopes for him. Occasionally, JW's mother would speak glowingly about EW as if he might be the first in the family to attain future success. I do know EW did pretty well in school, and never got into any real trouble. I believe EW's life was just beginning to take off when a tragedy occurred. During the beginning of my little league football training camp, JW got a hold of me and told me something terrible had happened to his brother. I couldn't imagine what he would tell me, but when he told me, I was shocked and saddened. Apparently, EW , who was with his girlfriend, started playing a Russian roulette-type of game with a gun. He didn't intent to hurt himself, but when he put the gun to his temple and pulled the trigger, he shot himself in the head.

EW's family was devastated. As a friend to JW , I wanted to support him the best I could. He wanted me to attend EW's funeral. Without a doubt, I was determined to go. However, my decision to go to EW's funeral put my little league football career in jeopardy. At the time, my head football coach, JC, was pretty tough. JC didn't tolerate kids missing too many practices, and I had already missed one. But I put the word out that I was going to miss practice and support my friend at his brother's funeral. When I returned to the team following the funeral, I was cut from the team (I rejoined the team the following year). Though disappointed, I was happy I made the decision to support JW. I can still see JW's mother weeping and broken at the funeral. JW tried to be strong, but it was too much to bear. In fact, I'm not sure this family was quite the same after EW's death.

Not long after these events, JW's mother had twins by a man who didn't stay around very long, and they continued to struggle financially. There was one positive thing that happened later in the year. JW and I were baptized together at my home church (we were around eleven years old) as we accepted and professed Jesus Christ to the congregation. It was a great moment for us; but because we were so young in need of much guidance and mentoring, I'm not sure we could fully appreciate all that this decision meant. After a few years, JW and I seemed to drift apart and go in different directions. By the time I reached high school, JW and his family had left the neighborhood and moved on. Every now and then, I'd hear something about JW or his family that led me to believe things weren't going well. Still, I carried much love in my heart for him and his family. As I sit here and think about my good friend who I haven't seen in over thirty years, I pray that he and his family were able to overcome all the negativity they faced in life.

In reflecting on "the very bad" aspects of my early years, my family and I lived in an environment where poverty, assault, abuse, murder, and tragedy took place. Living under these conditions made life hard; but we loved each other and tried to make it together through the minefield. We took the "very good" with the "bad" and the "very bad." Fortunately, God allowed the "very good" days to inspire my life and used the "bad" and "very bad" days to later transform me. As I previously mentioned, the Tate family adopted me, took the question mark off my life, and gave me love and a foundation. Had they not rescued me, only God knows where I would have ended up. Through it all, I spent seventeen years with these individuals. However, things would change. Up to this point, I had lost a family, gained a family and loved and lived with this family in a challenging environment. Now, I would discover what it meant to experience the greatest loss of my life.

I LOST AGAIN – THE GREATEST LOSS OF MY LIFE

Before 1979, if I was asked what losses or challenges impacted my life the most, I probably would have mentioned some of the events previously discussed. Although being adopted wasn't terribly painful (in light of the love I received from my true family—the Tate family), it did leave some questions in my mind and an unsettled feeling hidden in my soul. After all, why would my biological parents give up on me? Although this question surfaced to some degree in my young life, it did not reach the levels of being close to someone and then losing him or her. I did lose my aunt and grandfather when I was very young. But I hardly knew them. However, what I did learn about them made me miss not getting the chance to know them more. My aunt (on my mother's side) was a sweet, Christian woman with a gift to play the piano. When she was a little girl, she was accidentally shot by a police officer (who was pursuing a criminal) and was crippled for the remainder of her life. Although she was confined to a wheelchair, she was involved in her church and community. She died around 1963.

My grandfather was a quiet man who seemed disciplined and neat. From what I'm told, he was pretty strict with my dad and his brothers. I don't think Dad was particularly close to Granddad, but I know he respected him. Granddad saw a lot of change in the world from the time he was born until he passed away. I bet he had a lot of stories to tell. Sadly, I didn't get much of a chance to hear them. Granddad passed away some years after my aunt. The losses of DD, N, AW, and EW were not personal, but they did touch my life in different ways. The loss of my aunt and granddad were more personal, but not deeply personal because I didn't have a long, strong connection with them. Still, for me, this was all a part of living in the minefield. I had to grow up fast living in the minefield. But I could put all these things together, and they could not have impacted my life more than losing the center of my life—my mother.

May 18, 1979 started out as an ordinary day. It was a Friday, and the weather was nice outside. I was looking forward to going to school, coming home, contacting my girlfriend, and making plans for the weekend. I remember getting up, eating breakfast, talking to Mom, and walking to school. In the afternoon, while in English class, a call came to our classroom. I can't remember whether my friend DJ took the call or was told to escort me to the main office, but I went to the main office with my friend DJ and approached the counter in the main office. The woman at the counter confirmed who I was and directly told me, "Your mother is dead!" I remember falling to the floor, overwhelmed with grief. How can this be? What happened? What does this mean? I felt like someone had snatched my heart out of my chest and thrown it on the ground. I don't remember how I got to the hospital (DJ probably took me), but I remember meeting my father there and going into this room where they put my mother.

Dad was strong, but this had shaken him. He wasn't emotional or distraught. He was a World War II veteran, and he was determined to keep a brave face for his young son. But in his despair, I believe I heard my dad whisper, "What am I going to do?" As I went into this little white room, Mom lay still on a table with a white cloth over her body. She had dropped dead at the house, and they couldn't revive her on the way to the hospital. She had heart problems and high blood pressure. When Mom hit the floor, she bumped her head, and I could see a few scrape marks on her head. Here lay my mom, this sweet, precious soul who took me into her home and heart.

All my life, Mom was my anchor. She loved me, spoiled me, and was my biggest supporter. I'm sure I took her for granted at times, but I didn't know she would be leaving me so soon. I didn't know that Friday morning would be the last time I would see my mother alive. If I had known Mom was going to leave me that day, I would have wrapped my arms around her and never let go. At the hospital, I wanted to stay with her body and never leave her presence, but this was not possible. I remember touching my mother, kissing her, talking to her, and leaving. I felt like I was in a trance. I'd never been in this place before, and I didn't like it one bit. What kind of life was I supposed to live now? What would happen to my family and me? This new reality left me numb and unsure about the future.

When my dad and I left the hospital and went home, Maurice tried to be somewhat philosophical about Mom's death, but he was covering his true feelings. In fact, Maurice's life spun more and more out of control as a result of Mom's death. Billy tried to find comfort in the bottle, but the comfort he received was short lived. Ronnie was in jail and couldn't come to the funeral. But when I finally talked with him about our mother, he didn't show a lot of emotion. Perhaps he couldn't allow himself to feel the weight of the loss coupled with the reality that his life choices nullified him from paying his last respects to his mother. Chester was mentally ill, so he wasn't able to comprehend mother's death. Grandma was up in age, and unable to come to the funeral. But I know she was deeply hurt. Grandma had now outlived both of her daughters. When I talked to her, she kept a brave face. I know everybody was torn up about this, but I think I took it the hardest because I was the closest to her. Plus, when I did well in school, sports, or other activities, Mom was always so proud of me. It seemed like Mom lived to see me succeed and do well in life. Now, she was gone. From this point on, my life could be divided into two parts: before Mom and after Mom. On May 18, 1979, one month before I graduated from high school, time stood still. Now I had to learn how to live without her. As I continued the journey of life, I would come to know what it meant to live without other family members as well.

The Way It Is – gone but not forgotten

Learning to live without Mom wasn't easy, but it's a reality I had to face. She was gone, but would never be forgotten. Subsequently, between ages seventeen and forty-five, I lost everyone in my immediate family, plus some relatives. Sometimes when a person loses a loved one, a part of him or her dies as well. On the other hand, loss can challenge one to grow; to become more determined to live the best life possible; to have a greater appreciation for family and friends; and to reach out to others. As I reflect on learning to live without my loved ones, I'll discuss each family member and the time period of their death; what was going on with me and my life at the time of their death; the impact and my response to the family member's loss; and the aftermath.

Before I dive into my response to each of my family member's death, I'd like to offer these observations. Many factors contribute to how one may respond to loss. Some of those factors are how close one was to the loved one; one's age and maturity level at the time of loss; one's situation in life at the time of loss; one's belief about death and the afterlife; whether the loved one was young or old, suffered from an illness, or had his or her life cut short; how the loved one lived his or her life; and one's belief and support system in coping with loss.

MOM

As I mentioned earlier, I was seventeen years old and one month from graduating from high school when Mom passed away. I was also three or four months away from attending my first year of college at Ohio University. Before May 18, 1979, I was an A student, honor-roll recipient, popular in high school, and a young, confident individual with promise, ready to step out into the world. Shortly after May 18, 1979, I was shattered and broken; however, I did make an effort to move on. When I graduated in June, 1979, I was very pleased. My dad and Maurice were there. I'm sure they were proud; but it wasn't quite the same without Mom. After graduation, my dad and I visited my grandmother and relatives in Knoxville, Tennessee. It was the first time I saw them since my Mom's death.

When I talked to my grandmother, I couldn't help but cry. My mother looked just like my grandmother. Grandma was strong and sweet. She comforted me and told me it was going to be all right. I saw Chester and talked to Ronnie. Everything seemed so different and strange because I'd never been to Knoxville without Mom. This definitely took some getting used to. After spending some time in Knoxville, my dad and I came back home, and I spent the rest of the summer hanging out with my girlfriend, P, and preparing for college. When September rolled around, my dad shook my hand and wished me well, and I drove to college with a friend.

For most young people, the transition from high school to college is unique because it's the first time a young person is somewhat on his or her own—especially if one is attending a college out of town or staying on campus. College definitely was a unique transition for me because I would be away from family for the first time in my life. Plus, learning to go to school, work, and live in an unfamiliar environment took some getting used to. I tried to let Mom's death motivate me to do well, but her absence was daunting. Several of my high school friends attended college with me, so that was pretty cool. In fact, one of my best friends (WC) from high school was my roommate. We played basketball together, hung out, and made other friends. Grade wise, I did fairly well during my first year of college—not great but OK. Under different circumstances, I believe this could have been a good experience for me, but my heart just wasn't in it.

Life just didn't seem the same anymore. Achieving, pursuing goals, holidays, and my world just didn't seem to matter as much without Mom. After a year of college, I went back home and worked for a while. I even registered for classes at Cleveland State University, but I quickly pulled the plug on that decision. While I was deciding what to do with my life, Dad talked to me about joining the Army. Actually, I think Dad felt I should have gone to the Army instead of college. Dad would tell me that he didn't have the money to send me to school, that the Army was good for him, and would be good for me, and that it would help me grow up some more.

As the weeks and months went by, I started to become more comfortable with staying home, hanging out, and living in the minefield. However, Dad didn't let me get too comfortable. Although in his heart he wanted me there, he felt our environment had too many distractions, and I was better off making the most of my life somewhere else. Plus, he believed if I stayed around too long, I might get into trouble and mess up my life. So he kept talking to me about the military and doing something with my life. After talking with others and visiting a few military recruiters, I decided to join the Air Force. I signed up for the delayed enlisted program in January 1981 and left Cleveland for basic military training on March 25, 1981.

This was no small move for me because I never considered doing anything other than going to college. In fact, I never looked at the military as being a viable option for me. However, my life was in a different place now. I didn't have the concentration and motivation to be a full-time student, but I didn't want to end up with a dead-end job. Little by little, I was losing my edge to succeed. I needed to leave the minefield and experience something different. So, I thought, maybe Dad is right. Maybe, my life needs to go in a different direction—the military. After all, the military offers quite a bit. I could take college courses, learn a trade, and earn and save some money. Furthermore, I needed structure; the opportunity to grow and expand my mind; to be in a place where I could cultivate my skills and abilities; to be in a place where I could be away from the current distractions and not be allowed to run home quickly; and the opportunity to experience new challenges. Although I had this new vision for my life, everybody didn't necessarily see it this way. Because I had done so well in high school and seemed like the college type, some people were surprised by my decision to join the military—especially a few family members and close friends.

If I could read some of their minds, I sure I would hear them say, *Did he abandon his dreams too soon? Is he really cut out for the military? Does he really know what he's doing?* In spite of the questions that I felt lingered in the minds of some of my staunchest supporters, I headed off to San Antonio, Texas, to begin my military career. Of course, after my first day of basic training, I thought my decision was borderline lunacy. Jose Tate, the guy who woke up late in the morning and barely cleaned his room, was now doing things before the sun came up. During basic training, the Air Force took away our civilian clothes, cut our hair, gave us some funny-looking uniforms, and made us march, run, and salute on command.

They told us when to wake up and when to go to bed; when to eat; where we could go; how long we could talk on the phone; and how we needed to conduct ourselves. Naturally, at nineteen years old, I didn't see the genius of going through this experience; but later I could see how it helped developed my character. While in basic training, I was able to secure a future job in the medical administration field. After graduation, I went to Sheppard Air Force Base, Texas, to medical administration training school for four weeks. It was a less stressful environment than basic, and I was able to experience a little more freedom. In fact, things were going just fine until I got my first duty assignment.

While in basic training, trainees had to complete an assignment preference form, specifying bases one would prefer to be assigned. The common name for this form was a "dream sheet" because you would put down places you would hope and dream to go. On my "dream sheet," I put all stateside bases close to Ohio. Since Wright-Patterson Air Force Base was three or four hours from home, I thought this would be ideal. Unfortunately, I discovered another reason why people called this form a "dream sheet"—because you had to be dreaming if you thought you'd actually get what you put down on this form.

So one day, when a couple of friends and I heard our assignments were in, we went to our various stations to get our orders. When we gathered together and I read my orders, I didn't want to believe what I was seeing! On these orders, I saw the words "Incirlik Air Base, Turkey." Incirlik, Turkey? Someone made a big mistake. I didn't even put overseas bases on my dream sheet. How did this happen? When my so-called friends saw my response, they "gave me the business." Man, they laughed, joked, and made fun of the situation to the point I'm surprised one of them didn't pee in his pants. Later on, when I was by myself, I broke down. All kinds of negative thoughts crossed my mind: I lost my mother, what happens if I get over there and something happens to my dad; or what if I get over there and something goes wrong? Leaving home to go to Texas was the farthest I'd ever been from home by myself. Now, I was leaving the country to go somewhere I had barely heard of and didn't care to know. I called home and complained to my dad about the situation. I wanted my dad to call our local councilman, state representative, or somebody who could get me out of this situation. Of course, Dad wasn't buying this.

Dad wanted me to "man up," and do what the military was telling me to do. Over the next few weeks, he pulled out all the stops to shake me out of this negative state of mind. In one of his letters to me, he said, "If your mother knew what you were trying to do, she would turn over in her grave." And, "You're my only hope, so don't blow it. Think about the consequences before you do the wrong thing." His words lay heavily on my heart because I loved Mom too much to do anything I thought would hurt her, and I didn't want to let Dad down. However, Dad really hit me hard when he played the Christian card. Dad said, "You say you go to church and believe in the Bible. Then why are you so afraid, O ye of little faith? His eyes are on the sparrows, and I know He watches you!" He also advised me to go talk to my chaplain, tell him how I felt, and listen to him (in light of what I've become, I smile every time I think about this).

Frankly, Dad never broke things down like this. Before my mom's death, he was more reserved, less vocal, and definitely didn't talk much about spiritual matters. However, I believe my mother's passing raised his spiritual awareness and his need for God in his life. As a result, a new sheriff was in town, and Dad came at me full force. Between my Dad's words, encouragement from a trusted Christian instructor at tech school, and a slowly growing spiritual awareness, I found the strength to go to Turkey. When I got over there, I played with the medical unit football team and had a great first game before I broke my finger—

which ended my season. In fact, I had to go to Wiesbaden, Germany, to the Air Force Hospital to get pins put in my finger and later go back to get them taken out. I took college classes on base. I regularly attended church and later joined a small Christian group. My dad wrote me regularly, and I even called him when I could—though Dad was very adamant about me wasting my money (his words) talking long distance on the phone. Also, I got letters and cards from P, friends, and other family members. All in all, I did quite a bit of growing up over there. Again, Dad was right.

The next time the Air Force asked me to fill out a "dream sheet," I was told I had a better chance of getting what I wanted because Turkey was a remote assignment with a future base of preference (after successful completion of the assignment). Cautiously optimistic, I put down Wright-Patterson Air Force Base, Ohio, and I actually got it! In July 1982, I finished my time in Turkey, went home on leave, and prepared for my next assignment in Ohio. Dad welcomed me back home with open arms and told me how proud I made him. My family, friends, and neighbors were very affirming and glad to see me. Deep in my heart, I know Mom was proud of me too. Although, she wasn't there physically to welcome me home, my memory of her told me she was very happy my life was going in a positive direction. After weeks at home, I was off to Wright-Patterson Air Force Base, Ohio, to continue the journey.

DAD

I think it was after I came home from college, and before I joined the Air Force, that Dad confided in me that he was seeing a doctor for medical issues. Of course, Dad always downplayed his condition and rarely complained. In light of the passing of my mother, I'm sure he didn't want me to know the seriousness of his condition because I might worry. Yet, in my gut I always knew all wasn't well—another big reason why I was stressed about going overseas. Since Dad remained upbeat about his condition, I turned my attention to my life at Wright-Patterson Air Force Base. Actually, life was pretty good. My first year at Wright-Patterson Air Force Base, I lived in the dormitory. Then, I moved off base and rented an apartment in Dayton. I ate at the chow hall (free food), went to the gym and recreation center (free exercise and recreational services), and didn't have far to travel for work. My first job was in the mailroom, followed by medical records, and admissions and dispositions.

Sometime in September of 1982, a lady (AW) who worked at Wright-Patterson Medical Center (WPMC) invited me to her church. Soon, I became a member. This was a small Pentecostal church, quite different from the United Methodist and Baptist churches I had been exposed to growing up. However, since it did remind me of some of my more charismatic friends I worshipped with and hung out with in Turkey, I felt pretty comfortable. I particularly liked the energy of this church. Although services could be quite long, there was plenty of singing, dancing (in the spirit), testifying, and "letting the Lord have His way" (as some would say) in the service.

People seemed free to express their love and appreciation for God in a powerful way. No one appeared inhibited or shy about "praising the Lord." The experience was liberating! Soon, I caught the "spirit" and began to share in leading the devotional part of the service, and I also lead a Bible study. Suddenly, I found myself saying and doing things in church that I rarely did before—testifying, singing, dancing, leading Bible studies, praising God, and so forth. Plus, I developed some good relationships with several church members. This was definitely the "upside" of being a member of this spirited little Pentecostal church.

However, as time marched on, I discovered a few "challenges" to serving in this congregation. First, there were the implied, subtle messages concerning salvation, holiness, education (seminary or Bible college) and what it meant to be "right with God." Some people in the church believed that if a woman wore pants, she wasn't or couldn't be saved; that playing sports, listening to music (other than gospel or Christian music) and going to the movies was considered worldly and in conflict with being spiritual. Some referred to seminary as "the cemetery" because they believed you needed only the Holy Ghost for instruction, and the unspiritual or unsaved people in seminary could dilute one's faith, and some believed that few churches or people from other denominations were as holy, righteous, and loving as we were.

Sometimes these implied, subtle messages came from key (in my eyes) members within the congregation. Since the church's core belief system was based on the life, death, burial, and Resurrection of Jesus Christ, I wasn't overly concerned with "sideline" interpretations of God's Word and the Christian life. Plus, I was well aware that within any congregation, people are at different levels or places regarding their faith. Still, I was pretty young in the faith and impressionable. So when certain individuals exalted us above the Baptists (who were sometimes characterized as folks who didn't mind doing a little drinking and smoking on the side), Methodists (not very spiritual), and others, it caused me to sub-conscientiously think more highly of "us" and less of "them."

Furthermore, as I listened to these messages and observed the rhetoric communicated about what it means to be "holy," the grace of

God seemed to give way to feeling that one never could quite measure up. In my mind, the emphasis always seemed bent toward performance and perfection instead of God loving you where you are and helping you to become what He wants you to be. The idea that spiritual growth and maturity takes time seemed to evade some in the congregation. In retrospect, the theology that many embraced in this church was unbalanced and too idealistic. However, it didn't seem to take away church members' hunger and love for God (as they understood Him) or the kind, loving acts many members showed toward others.

Overall, these were good, loving, imperfect, church people, striving to understand and serve a holy, righteous God. In addition, I'm sure the promotion of "living holy" helped many not to live a sloppy, undisciplined, carnal life or "play church." Yet this attitude did make it challenging understanding God's grace, mercy, forgiveness, and how much He really loves us. In fact, I unknowingly began to take on a critical, judgmental spirit. Sure, I could be kind and support others. But there were other times I saw life as black and white with little middle ground—little room for error. In other words, one was either in or out, saved (and doing everything right) or unsaved (lost, and yielding to temptation or sin), spiritual (on fire for the Lord) or carnal (doing one's own will instead of God's will, which was often defined by others).

Sure, in the strictest sense, one could argue that the Bible supports these claims. However, spiritual truths from the Bible such as "The Lord is merciful and gracious, slow to anger, and abounding in mercy" (Psalm 103:8), "But when He (Jesus) saw the multitudes, He was moved with compassion for them, because they were weary and scattered, like sheep having no shepherd" (St. Matthew 9:36), and "He (God) who is in you is greater than he who is in the world" (I John 4:4) are truths for flawed human beings in need of love, grace, and hope. All of these things notwithstanding, the implied, subtle message that would ultimately affect me the most was "if you were prayed up, living in accordance to God's word, and really spiritual, you wouldn't suffer like others." In other words, if God isn't moving in your life in a powerful way, you must be doing something wrong. And if you experience too much pain and suffering in life, you're definitely doing something wrong (similar to what Job's friends expressed to him in Job chapters 4–12). Though I never totally accepted these convictions concerning the amount of suffering being a barometer for one's spiritual life, in 1984, my faith was really put to the test. Soon, I would learn that Dad was dying.

In February 1984, I called home to talk to Dad to see how he was doing. My brother Maurice answered the phone, and was very evasive about Dad. The more Maurice talked, the more I felt something was wrong. Finally, I pressed him to tell me exactly what was going on, then he told me the truth—Dad was sick in the hospital. My heart sank to the ground. Immediately, I thought, "I've got to get home to be with my Dad." After talking with my brother, I informed my superiors about this situation and went home.

When I made it home, I immediately went to see Dad at the hospital. I remember entering the hospital room and seeing something strange in this bed that was supposed to be occupied by my father. Before I entered this room, I always had a strong, positive image of my Dad. Dad always seemed physically and emotionally strong—rolling with the punches of life and bouncing back from adversity. However, today was a new day. When I walked into this room, I saw a frail, weak man holding on to life. I could almost feel myself backing up a bit as I got closer to him, but I did not want to appear too overwhelmed by the moment. When I reached my father, I collapsed on him with love and concern.

As I held my dad, he acknowledged me but remained still and kept his composure as if to say, *Son, I've still got to be strong for you.* Dad was old school. He wasn't as emotional and transparent as I have been in my life, and he didn't always share his pain or concerns. But I could tell the end was in sight. Dad and I talked for a day or so before he lost his reasoning skills and consciousness. One day when my friend DJ and I were visiting Dad, Dad started talking about seeing things in the room. DJ was very kind and thoughtful not to make anything of this during or after visiting Dad. Shortly, after this episode, my dad began to slip out of consciousness.

On one of my last visits before the end, I saw him with this glazed look in his eyes and breathing heavily. I was so shocked and dismayed that I asked one of the medical people what was going on, and he gestured with his finger (making circles around his temple area), suggesting that Dad was crazy—in front of another employee. At the time, his insensitive and unprofessional response to my wounded soul did not fully register with me. I saw him and the shocked look of his coworker regarding his response, but my mind and heart were someplace else. I didn't fully realize it at the time, but God was carrying and shielding me as I went through this experience.

Much later, upon reflection, I did recall this moment, and it saddened me how uncaring and out of touch people can be—especially a health care worker. I'm sure this moment played a major role in the type of care and compassion I would later give in serving others. Nevertheless, I got through that moment and continued to be with Dad (every day) until the day we got that unwanted call from the hospital—*I'm sorry, Mr. Tate has died.*

Dad's dead. I couldn't believe it. Only less than five years prior to this, my family and I buried my mother. Now we were saying good-bye to another pillar in my life. Though I was not his blood son, he treated me as (if not more than) a son. This man gave me his last name, raised me, put a roof over my head, food on my table, and clothes on my back. He encouraged, supported, and loved me. He helped me through one of the most difficult, painful moments in my life (the death of my mother), and refused to let me throw my life away. He could have been compromising in bidding me to remain at home and stay by his side when he too was hurting from losing the love of his life. Or he could have hit the road, bailed out, and left me to fend for myself. But his love for me compelled him to push me out of the nest, help me to stand on my own two feet, and be a man. What a father! What a man! Again I say, what a father!

I'm eternally grateful to have the parents I had. Mom and Dad were not perfect, but they were perfect for me! I would not trade them for anyone or anything. Their love and support outweighed their shortcomings. And their lives outweighed their deaths. Who they were and what we shared together still speaks to me today. I'm so grateful God (through His mercy and kindness) chose to give me these individuals. I'm comforted in the knowledge that their legacy lives on in and through me. I celebrate them. I honor them. And I love them still.

It's tough to lose your parents at any age, but I never imagined I would lose both of my parents before I turned twenty-three years old. Nevertheless, this was my reality, and I had to deal with it. During this time, I turned to God, church, family, and friends. After burying Dad and spending time with family and friends, I headed back to Wright-Patterson Air Force Base. Little did I know, I would soon return.

MAURICE

When I got back to Dayton and resumed my life, I had moments when I thought about the impact of my parents' death on the family. In retrospect, though I struggled with the loss of both parents, I used positive and spiritual resources to help me cope with my new reality. On the other hand, my brothers were attracted to less admirable resources in dealing with their hurt and pain. Besides keeping things on the inside and repressing their feelings, Billy and Maurice used the bottle, weed, or other unhealthy means to self-medicate, and Ronnie continued his dealings in the streets. Although I loved my brothers very much, I knew I couldn't change them. In fact, one episode after my father's passing almost got me clobbered.

The day my dad died, Billy, his friends, and I were in the house discussing the events that just took place. My brother seemed a little tipsy, and I thought I smelled alcohol coming from him. I confronted him about it in front of his friends! Big mistake! I'm not sure if this was temporary insanity or just plain stupidity, but my response to my older brother ("scrap iron," who could dust you off in a blink of an eye) came out of feeling his actions were unsuitable for the situation at hand. After I spoke out against him, Billy was hot! He looked at me like a lion about to devour his prey and gave me a few choice words before his friends intervened. For a split second, I saw something in my brother's eyes that I had never, ever seen before. At this moment, I realized I had gone too far, and I quickly embraced my brother and apologized profusely to him.

Back in the day, if I had dreamed of talking to my brother this way, I would have woken up and smacked myself! He was definitely not the one you confronted this way—sober or not! Fortunately, Billy forgave me. In fact, after he thought about it, I know he felt bad about how he handled the situation. However, I needed to use better judgment and realize people don't always handle adversity the way you hope they would. Yes, he was my older brother, and I had realistic expectations of him in terms of how he conducted himself during this challenging moment in our lives. But losing a loved one affects people and family members in different ways. Whether or not people have good coping skills, and support may determine how they deal with the loss.

Due to my maturity level and dealing with my own feelings about the situation, I could not step back and see how the situation was affecting him. The issue was not about condoning his behavior or making excuses in my own mind about his choice to drink during this time, but my goal should have been not adding fuel to the fire—making things worse. Sometimes, using wisdom in a situation is better than being "right." I learned a valuable lesson that would serve me well later in life as a chaplain and caregiver in terms of meeting people where they are instead of where you want them to be.

As much as Billy may have struggled with the passing of our parents, Ronnie and Maurice didn't seem to struggle much outwardly. But, deep down inside, I sensed that Maurice struggled more than Billy and Ronnie. I remember during the same period after my father died, my brothers and cousin (who were near my dad's age and favored him) had a meeting at our house. During this meeting, my cousin L was very negative toward Maurice and really came down on him. L did not come around very often, and he definitely never talked about my brother to me in this fashion. Nevertheless, as I mentioned before, people deal with death in different ways. However, I think this occasion gave L a venue to express what he really thought of Maurice.

You see, in L's eyes, Maurice never amounted to much. So I guess he felt it was his duty to demoralize my brother in front of the rest of us. Neither Maurice nor the rest of my brothers said anything; but when I looked at Maurice, I could tell L's words pierced his soul. I spoke up and voiced my displeasure (there I go again). However, this time my righteous indignation was more appropriate in reproving my cousin and supporting my brother instead of being too critical and judgmental. After my reproving of L, he stopped dogging Maurice, and we continued with the meeting. Fortunately, we went on to bury my father with dignity. Again, it seemed everyone had his or her own way of dealing with losses in our family. Some ways were good, and some were not so good. This was definitely a rough period for all of us. My hope and prayer was that we would all make it through this strange place in life without falling to pieces. Unfortunately, things got a lot worse before they would get any better.

In April, less than two months after we buried my father, I got a call from Ronnie that Billy had died. I was floored. Then, Ronnie called back and told me it wasn't Billy, but it was Maurice! Somehow, Ronnie got things mixed up. Nevertheless, I learned I just lost a brother and lost him in the most horrific way. He told me someone murdered him! Murdered? I couldn't believe my ears. Who would want to murder my brother? Maurice was a gentle soul. He was a people pleaser and too trusting, but he would not hurt a fly.

Maurice might have stayed too long in the 1960s, wasn't very ambitious, and liked some of the pleasures of life a bit too much, but he certainly didn't deserve to have his life taken. To make matter worse, my brother was not only murdered, but was savagely murdered! Ronnie told me Maurice was stabbed over twenty five times and beaten with a blunt object over twenty times. His blood was splattered all over the floors and the walls. Ronnie said the killer(s) murdered Maurice and ransacked the house. No one was charged with the murder—although Maurice's so called friend LR (who was the last person to leave the house shortly before my brother's murder) was questioned by the police.

Billy had the unfortunate task of identifying my brother's body—a devastating thing to have to endure. As soon as Ronnie told me this, I contacted the church mother who offered support. Also, she asked me to call one of the ministers for counseling and support. The pastor must have been unavailable at the time, so I called Brother minister and told him what had happened. I liked Brother minister and had received helpful insights from his ministry on other occasions. But this situation proved to be somewhat different. Brother minister offered something along the lines of "Well, I guess that should teach us to pray for our family." Then, he proceeded with other words that fell on deaf ears. Wow! Was he suggesting that my prayer or spiritual life (as if he really knew what my prayer or spiritual life really was) played a part in my brother's demise? This was the classic "friends of Job" response (from the book of Job in the Bible) when Job faced calamities. Job's friends surmised that Job must have done something wrong to experience the trauma and tragedy he faced. They determined that bad things don't happen to people in right relationship with God. So they thought it was a smart idea to reprove an individual who had already lost almost everything he had; was afflicted with boils and sores all over his body; and whose wife told him to curse God and die. And they did this all in the name of the Lord! Well, down the road, God reeducated and reproved Job's friends for their impractical and damaging theology (as I'm sure God corrected Brother minister for his "out of touch" theology).

Throughout my ministry, I've heard people talk of how they left the church because someone hurt them, was a bad role model, or didn't support them. Sometimes I share this story (and others as well because I do have a few) and tell them not to give up on God because none of us is perfect. We should never confuse God with the church, even though the church is called to a higher standard of living and of handling situations. Often, I go on to say, we must rely more on who God is and the mercy, grace, strength, and love God has for us, as opposed to relying on imperfect church folk (including my imperfect self) who are limited. Though his words were tough to hear, I didn't let his theology or assessment of my spirituality stop me from embracing a more loving, comforting God. In fact, his words didn't hurt me as much as one might think because God didn't let it. In the long run, I think the experience taught me what not to do or say than anything else. I forgave him years ago for his lack of empathy and wisdom in how to appropriately bring healing and comfort to one dealing with death and tragedy. Forgiveness becomes more important for the one needing to forgive than for the transgressor.

After I gathered myself in talking to Brother minister, I took care of a few things and headed to Cleveland. Shortly, Billy, his friend, and I went to the house to clean it up. We had to clean Maurice's blood off the floors and the walls, and straighten up the house. Soon, we had to make funeral arrangements; but the back of Maurice's head was beaten in so severely, funeral preparations took longer than anticipated. When Maurice was prepared for viewing, he had a veil over his casket covering his head area to protect anyone from seeing the damage done to him. Shortly before, during, and after the funeral, LR was acting very strange, as if he were guilty or trying to hide something. In fact, one of Maurice's friends said he saw LR rushing from my brother's house that night but couldn't confirm whether this was in connection with my brother's murder. I don't think LR offered much help to the police either (concerning what he saw). To this day, I've never confronted LR about his involvement in my brother's death, but different people shared interesting tidbits about my brother's relationship with him that caused me to wonder about his friendship with my brother. Whoever did this unthinkable evil was never caught, tried by a jury, or punished (as far as I know unless God punished him) for their crimes.

At the gravesite as the family stood by Maurice's casket upon the preacher's last words before dismissal, I remember seeing tears flowing down Billy's face. This was the first time I ever saw Billy cry. It took a lot to make him cry. What a sad situation! Now, I've lost two important people in my life within two months. One dies of cancer, and another is brutally murdered like an animal! When my mother passed away, it was unexpected. But I knew deep inside my heart Mom was a Christian who would live eternally with Jesus. Likewise, when Dad died less than two month ago, I knew he had grown stronger spiritually and would no longer suffer anymore from cancer. Maurice was not suffering from any disease nor was he a dying old man who had lived a full life. He was only thirty-one years old! Though a friend did tell me (without my prodding) Maurice was seeking spiritual guidance after my Dad's death, I wondered if he accepted the Lord as his personal savior and made peace with God before he left this earth. I can only hope and pray that he did.

Not knowing if one's loved one made peace with God or accepted God's plan of salvation before death is not an easy subject to contemplate—especially if there were little to no outward signs the person did so. Nobody wants to think his or her loved one will suffer eternally. So what do I tell myself? What do I chose to believe? I could have told myself some of the things I've heard people say, such as "God is too good and caring to allow anyone to suffer eternally," or "Hell and damnation are reserved only for the devil and his demons." Or "Even if we get it all wrong in this life, we'll get another chance or numerous chances somewhere down the road (after this life) to get it right and live in peace eternally." No, I chose to turn my thoughts, questions, and concerns over to God.

Fortunately, God gave me a truth about this complex situation that has grown and expanded over the years. I've learned that I don't have to fabricate or make up things to appease myself because I'm not in control of the order of life and cannot dictate where one spends eternity. This type of control and power is reserved for the Creator of all things and Giver of life, who is much higher and greater than anyone. Plus, I realize my human view and understanding is limited, biased, and tainted. God's truth is better than anything I (or anyone else) can conjure up or mastermind; and His truth has the ability to give one freedom.

Through God's wisdom, I've come to believe these things: 1) God is a God of love, mercy, compassion, forgiveness, grace, and judgment; 2) It is more important to focus on what my departed loved ones meant to me and how I will continue to love, honor, and celebrate their lives instead of agonizing over where they may spend eternity; and, 3) I can learn much from my departed loved one's life and death. Let me further explain by starting with the first point.

God is a balanced God but leans toward mercy (For God so loved the world…St. John 3:16). For me, God isn't an almighty Supreme Being eagerly waiting to knock us over the head and send us off to hell. Nor is God a genie in a bottle ready to accommodate our every desire and demand. I've learned that the world doesn't center on me (or any human being); but I'm better off if my world is centered on Him. Furthermore, I'm convinced the Scriptures depict a God who greatly loves His creation; longs to be in relationship with His creation; makes provisions for His creation; and requires His creation to be in relationship with Him. The Bible tells us that God loves us with an unconditional love, saves us by His grace (and not by our works), and has a mercy that endures forever! Yet God did not create us to be robots, and has given us "free will."

The Bible tells us in St. John 3:17, "For God sent his Son (Jesus) into the world, not to condemn the world, but to save the world." So God's desire for humanity is not condemnation, but salvation—not to separate Himself from us but to invite us to live together forever with Him! And if God's mercy endures forever, His grace is amazing, and His love covers a multitude of sins, I know He loves humanity (especially me) in spite of our shortcomings! It doesn't mean there are no consequences for the choices one makes or the life one chooses to live; it means that God is committed to His creation far more than we (with our limited minds) can ever know. Therefore, I leave my brother in the hands of a loving, merciful, just, balanced God whose wisdom far exceeds mine and whose judgment is supreme.

In regard to my second point (celebrate loved ones' lives instead of agonizing where they may spend eternity), I can almost hear someone saying, "Am I supposed to ignore the fact that if my loved one didn't live a Christian/religious life, he or she will be judged? And how can I just love my loved ones if I don't believe they made it to heaven?" I'm not suggesting that one ignore the departed loved one's belief system or the life he or she led on earth. For me, it's a matter of focusing on what I can control and how I want to continue loving a departed loved one.

I could not control Maurice's life or the decisions and choices he made. And I had no control over where he might spend eternity. But

I can think about the times we shared, what he meant to me, and how I want to keep him in my memory and heart. I can thank God I had a brother at all because God didn't have to allow me to have him. I can think about him throughout the day and focus on the positive things he added to my life. I can celebrate his life by keeping his memory alive and sharing his life with others. And I can reflect upon his personality and things he would say to me when he was at his best and draw inspiration from him.

In reply to my last point, (I can learn from his life and death), my brother's life has taught me how fragile life is and how important it is to make each day count. Life is too short, and nothing is promised. We're not promised we'll live on earth a hundred years, be rich and famous, never get sick, or never face painful situations. We're imperfect human beings living in a fallen world, destined to leave it. No one can stay beyond the time God has set for one to stay. Yet we can learn how to make the best of our human situation.

I'm sure if my brother were physically here, he would tell me that many things he thought mattered don't matter as much now. And I'm sure he would tell me to focus on the things that matter and give myself totally to them—striving and living the life God has called us to live. In many ways, this is what his life tells me to this day. I need this message because sometimes I get distracted and lose focus (as we all do). And I need to be reminded to stay on course so I will live a life that counts.

In conclusion, these are the things I learned from God concerning Maurice. As long as I live, my brother's life will never be in vain. He touched people's lives, made people laugh, and was loved much by his family and friends. Now, it's just Billy, Ronnie, Chester, and me. We had to work through these losses, regroup, and continue the journey of life. I prayed for God's healing and help in moving forward. After my brother's funeral, I visited with family, friends, and headed back to Dayton. It would be another four years (1988) before I buried another member of my family.

GRANDMA

A few years before my dad and brother passed away, my grandmother and Chester both went to a nursing home and health care facility. Grandma was a wonderful grandmother. In fact, we used to affectionately call her "Little Mother." She came from a multicultural background. She had long, pretty hair, adorable eyes, a beautiful smile, olive skin, and a small frame. During the time my father and brother passed away, she was eighty-eight years old. "Little Mother" lived longer than her daughters, son-in-law, and grandson. She was a strong, Christian woman who had seen and experienced a lot in her lifetime. Throughout her life, she lived in a world that wasn't very kind or accepting of her. Often, she struggled to make ends meet and the conditions of her times made it hard for her to advance. Still, she had a heart of gold and never displayed any bitterness or bias.

She took care of Chester, raised Ronnie, and was very loving to her family. I remember when I was a kid growing up, "Little Mother" would send me money on my birthday and Christmas. When she would send me dimes in aluminum foil, it made me feel like I hit the jackpot. Not only did she send me gifts, it was a gift to be around her. When my mom and I visited her, I always felt like I was right at home. She was always supportive and encouraging. Like my mom, "Little Mother" had a special place in her heart for me. The good times I shared with her would serve me well in the years before God called her home. In 1982, when my dad wrote me that "Little Mother" and Chester had to be placed in a care facility, he told me "Little Mother" had become sick, forgetful, and could no longer take care of Chester. Of course, I was very saddened to learn this about her, but I knew God and other family nearby would keep watch over her. However, her condition got worse; and as time moved on, "Little Mother" was diagnosed with Alzheimer's disease. Eventually, Alzheimer's disease stole her memory of me and a big portion of her life. I found this to be true when my nephew (who is around a decade younger than I) and I visited her at her nursing facility.

At this time, "Little Mother" was around ninety years old. But, in her mind, she was living in the 1930s. I remember walking into her room with my nephew (CD), giving her a hug and a kiss, and sitting down to talk to her. We told her who we were, asked how she was doing, and began to try to connect with her. "Little Mother" was very kind and sweet as usual, but she couldn't recall who we were. I told her I was "Baby Doll's son" (Baby Doll was my mother's nickname) and talked to her about some other family members. "Little Mother" talked about my mother and aunt, but she talked about them when they were very young. Also, she talked about the times she lived in and certain events that took place. It broke our hearts to see her this way. So after we talked, I asked if we could pray for her. "Little Mother" loved the idea of us praying, so we began to pray.

During our prayer, I heard my nephew say something similar to, "God, why is this happening to us?" Although I never heard my nephew express himself like this, I felt his pain. We both bore our souls in ways we had not done before. It was a profound moment, indeed. After we prayed, "Little Mother" looked at us like she didn't know what was going on but was glad we were there. After my nephew and I embraced her and said our good-byes, we departed. When we were alone, we talked about what happened, embraced, and moved on. I continued to visit with family for several weeks, and then I traveled back home. When I got back to Dayton, I resumed my normal, everyday life.

At this point (summer of 1986), I had moved up a little in rank, had taken college courses, and was active in church (I joined a new church in 1985). For the most part, I was managing well and staying true to my faith. But I was unaware of a growing loneliness and vulnerability developing inside. I missed my departed loved ones more than I realized, and I wasn't really close with anybody. Slowly, this need to be connected in a meaningful relationship and have my own family began to dominate my thoughts. Since I hadn't dated or been in relationship with anybody for a couple of years, I became more open to moving forward with this part of my life.

Toward September, I began dating someone I worked with during Vacation Bible School; and in the spring of 1987, we were married. As I reflect upon my disposition after my Tennessee visit to this point in my life, I understand myself much better now and how events affected me and influenced my decisions to marry and so forth. All of life's events, no matter how big or small, fruitful or unfruitful, aren't wasted if we can learn from them. And the Christian/religious person or the "got-it-all-together" person (if there's such a creature) can learn more about himself or herself and how things affect him or her if they take the time to do so. A year after my marriage, I was off to Tennessee again. Only this time, the circumstances were much more deflating and sad.

"Little Mother" had passed away at ninety-two years old. In one sense, I was glad that she was no longer in the physical and mental condition she had dealt with for several years, and I was happy she was going on to be with the Lord (whom she received as a child). "Little

Mother" had lived a long time, experienced much, and left her legacy for us to embrace. I'm encouraged and empowered by her life, strength, and will to persevere through life's challenges. If anyone ever had a right to complain about being dealt a bad hand, she would have been justified in doing so. But she didn't complain or give in to negativity. She remained faithful, consecrated, and caring to the end. Someone once said, "Success is not measured solely by what one attains. It is measured by what one had to overcome to attain it." My grandmother was not a prominent, worldwide figure. Few outside her family, friends, neighbors, and church knew her. She did not capture the attention of others, as did Mother Teresa, Florence Nightingale, or Coretta Scott King. But in her own right, she was an amazing woman. Everyone should have a "Little Mother" in his or her life—a woman who is committed, long-suffering, optimistic, encouraging, caring, and godly. I know that I'm a better person for having her in my life. In 1988, I had to bid farewell to a cherished loved one. In less than two years, I would have to do the same again.

BILLY

After my daughter was born, I remember taking the family (along with some friends) to visit Billy in Cleveland. When Billy first saw my daughter, his face seemed to light up. I remember him gently touching her and saying something that made me laugh. Since Billy was sort of a "man's man," strong (in the physical sense) guy, I rarely saw him display this type of affection. When I was a little kid, Billy's affection for me was an occasional thump on the head, which caused me much consternation. Actually, Billy was a caring guy. He cared about his family and friends, but he had his own way of showing it. Also, growing up, I often thought of Billy as my defender. You know, in the neighborhood, it could get pretty rough. In the back of my mind, I knew if it got too rough, I could call on my big brother, and he would take care of business!

As I mentioned earlier, Billy had received the nickname, "scrap iron," and was known to open up a can of whoop (you know what) on an individual causing trouble. I didn't involve him much in my affairs (as defender), but on the one or two occasions that I did, he came through (not necessarily knocking someone's lights out, but handling the situation). I remember one situation (when I was a kid) that I will never forget. One day, when Ronnie and his family were visiting us for the summer, I took Ronnie's stepson to the store. While in the store, a kid tried to start a fight with him. During the ruckus, a much older guy (possibly a young adult) jumped into the mix, adding to an already volatile situation. As things got heated, I took him out of the store, and we began to walk home. Meanwhile, this guy became more agitated and began walking behind us, inciting him to come back and fight. Soon, we reached home, and I summoned my brother. Not only did Billy respond, but also Ronnie and Dad came out locked and loaded, which almost gave Mom a heart attack. The look on the guy's face was like "Oh crap, I've gone and done it now!" Fortunately, they were able to talk things out, and no one was hurt. This was an unusual encounter for my family because I never saw my brothers or Dad operate in this fashion, though I knew Billy could go there. Needless to say, we never had any trouble from this individual again. And, for a good while, I didn't have too much trouble from anyone.

Yes, Billy had a reputation, but his greatest gift was humor. Billy was very funny—at least I thought so. He just had a way of putting things that made me laugh, even when I didn't want to. I remember when I was a teenager home from college; I was talking to Billy about my life (staying in college or going to the military) when my girlfriend (P) became the topic. She was a sweet girl, and I really cared for her at that time. Billy, family members, and friends close to our family knew her and liked her, but several people questioned whether this relationship was in my best interest since I was trying to better myself, leave the minefield, and move on with my life. So, every now and then, I got some very subjective feedback about our relationship. However, I never heard Billy say a negative word about her until now.

After Billy grilled me about wanting to go into the military, he slipped (at least I think he slipped) and called my girlfriend a derogatory name. I think he was surprised he actually said it. I said something like, "No, you just didn't call her a %#@!*." He laughed, added a little humor, and tried to backtrack by saying he didn't call her this name. I wanted to be mad, but I had to hold back a little laughter inside because I knew he didn't mean it. If anything, he was more concerned about my life choices than ever hurting me or disrespecting her. I came away thinking, my brother is a "trip."

No matter the situation, I knew my brother cared. Also, I knew my brother struggled and was very complex (like most of us). He was strong, yet weak; humorous, yet sad; and helpful, yet unable to help himself. Someone once said, "We all have our demons." Being a Christian man and minister, I know the devil's job is to "steal, kill, and destroy" (St. John 10:10). And if this statement implies that the devil tries to create conflict, chaos, confusion, self-hate, and destruction in the lives of human beings, then I concur with the statement, "We all have our demons."

If alcohol is a vehicle the devil uses to cloud one's judgment, cause one to act outside his or her better self, trick one into retreating from reality into a false world of self-medication and denial, and addict the body and mind into thinking it needs alcohol more than the sober lifestyle God created all of us to live and enjoy, then my brother struggled with this demon. As I stated earlier, I do believe Billy had a problem with alcohol. But, after Mom died, his struggles seemed to get worse.

In addition to having triple bypass surgery prior to our mom's departure, Billy's life choices were having a negative effect on his body. For several years leading to my brother's final days, I would see the controlling and declining effect this substance had on him. If I would take a week and use it as an example of Billy's bout with alcohol, I would describe it as this: alcohol use on Monday; sick on Tuesday and Wednesday; feeling better on Thursday and Friday; back at it on Saturday; and sick again on Monday and Tuesday—only to go through this scenario again and again. It may not have played out verbatim this way, but during the latter part of his life, this seemed very close to reality.

Often, when I went to visit him, he would be in one of these stages. I would go up to his room (a house he shared with others), and see him struggle. On different occasions, I remember him throwing up in a bucket, shaking, or just looking and feeling terrible. However, my brother's plight didn't stop me from making my way to see him or care about him. You know, the funny thing about real love is, it gives one the ability to go the extra, extra mile. Some folks in and out of my family told me I should forget about my brothers, write them off because none of them seemed to measure up. But I never accepted that! Something inside of me kept me coming back. Something inside motivated me not to give up on my brothers, and I'm sure that someone was God! When I look back over my relationship with Billy, I'm glad I didn't give up on him or abandon him because he didn't measure up in some people's eyes. I have no regrets in that area. And if people thought that being present in his life was condoning or excusing his lifestyle, then they were misguided. In retrospect, I believe the Bible verse in I Corinthians 13:7–8a (describing love) best summarizes my actions and feelings toward Billy: "(Love) bears all things, believes all things, hopes all things, endures all things. Love never fails." I just tried to love my brother and stay positive and hopeful. Although there was no failing in our love for one another, I saw little change.

In mid-January, 1990, my niece (Billy's daughter) found Billy dead at his residence. When a friend of my brother called me with the news, I was shocked. He was only in his mid-fifties. The year 1990 turned out to be a year of endings. I lost my brother, and my marriage ended. Fortunately, I didn't lose my faith. Sometimes weak, sometimes strong, I refused to let go of God's unchanging hand. Despite the pain, God was still in control, and He continued to pour out His mercy, grace, and love to me. Billy was gone, but not forgotten. Like Maurice, I hope he made peace with God. I pray that in his final days and hours on earth, he talked to God and let God talk to him. I hope he came to see and accept Jesus as his Lord and Savior. Although I wasn't with him, God was there. I believe God stretched out His hand to him because (as I've mentioned before) it's in God's nature to save. Still, it was Billy's choice, and his alone. Love compels me to remain hopeful and keep pressing forward. I will continue to celebrate, honor, and highly value Billy's life and memory along with those of my other deceased family members. In a couple of years, I married again (we've been married for twenty years!), and lost my father-in-law within a year of our marriage. After losing Billy, it would be a few short years before I lost another brother.

CHESTER

The year was 1995, and I hadn't been to Tennessee in a while. Ronnie was still doing his thing, but Chester wasn't getting any better. While he was in a health care facility, he had taken a few falls and had sustained some injuries. Since Ronnie and nearby loved ones kept watch over Chester, I knew he was looked after. Still, I wish I could have played a greater role in Chester's life. He was a lot older than I was and under the care of someone his whole life. Although Chester's mental state was that of a very young child, he was a man (in terms of age) when I was a child. Still, when I was young, it was fun to be around Chester because he had a good heart and a lot of energy.

After "Little Mother" died, I didn't get back that way as often as I would have liked. Ronnie did manage to come up my way (on his way to going somewhere else) and visit. But Ronnie and I communicated mainly on the phone. When we did get the chance to talk, he would let me know how Chester was doing. Another thing that seemed to happen after my grandma died, time seemed to move very quickly and I experienced a lot of change in my life.

By 1995, I was no longer an enlisted man. I was an officer (second lieutenant) in the United States Air Force Chaplain Candidate Program—a reserve-training program for seminarians interested in becoming Air Force chaplains. Also, late in 1995, I became an ordained minister. For several years, I sensed God preparing me to accept His call to ministry. But, frankly, I didn't always feel I measured up! Dealing with life and myself kept me from fully embracing the life God had in store for me. Finally, when I realized God's call to ministry was more about God's purpose for my life than adversity or my perfection, I said "yes" to His will.

Having received my bachelor's degree in 1989 and being mentored by my chaplain/pastor while attending chapel on base, I accepted my call to ministry in 1992. Also, in that same year, I enrolled in a Master's of Divinity Program at a local seminary. As I sought God's will for my life, He gave me a vision for ministry in the Air Force as a chaplain. Because lay ministers can't receive ordination in the chapel setting, I soon joined a local Baptist church (with my chaplain/pastor's blessings). In April 1993, I preached my trial sermon and was licensed to preach. I continued working during the day (active duty) and taking classes after work until I left active duty and was accepted in the chaplain candidate program (March, 1994).

I was a full-time seminary student living on campus with my wife and stepdaughter; a chaplain candidate; a chaplain intern (at a local hospital); and an associate minister at my church. My plate was full! So 1994 came and went pretty fast. As I entered 1995, it was going pretty fast as well until I got a call about my brother. Chester had passed away. After receiving the call, I made preparations to travel to Tennessee.

I drove down to Tennessee, buried my third brother, visited family, and came back home. In reflection, Chester's death touched me in a different way than the others. I thought about his life and purpose on earth. Although Chester was not capable of choosing what type of life he would live, his life touched those who loved him. Someone might ask, "If he could not talk, think, or act in a rational way, what was his purpose? What was God's plan in creating him and allowing him to spend all of his days in this mental state on earth?" I would say to those who ask that I don't claim to have all the answers or know all the deep things of God, but I do know one thing, "God's gifts come in many packages." And, if God's gifts come in many packages, we must receive, love, cherish, respect, and handle with care every package that God creates and delivers to us!

Chester's purpose was his Creator wanted him here. His Creator made him a human being with special needs. Nevertheless, God created him both human and special. Perhaps, part of God's purpose in creating Chester and allowing him to live life in his condition was to remind us to treat all living souls with dignity and respect—especially those who are unable to take care of themselves. In life, it's very easy to overlook people who don't fit our mold or expectations. I don't know what it was like to be inside Chester's world, but we made our connections. Chester never had a chance to hang out with friends, go to school, graduate, get a job, drive a car, travel, date, go to the movies or a ball game, marry, raise children, or do the many things we often take for granted.

Chester was a big guy who towered over both my mother and grandmother. I'm not sure when my grandmother took over raising Chester. But I know they fed him, washed him, clothed him, talked to him, loved him, and took care of him. And I know "Little Mother" took care of him into her advanced years until her body and mind failed her. God bless her richly for her unconditional love and commitment to my brother! Although it was not easy to take care of Chester, he was special to all of us. I will remember his smile, laughter, and ability to enjoy some of the simpler things of life. He was my brother, and he was unique. I'm glad God created Chester and gave him to us. I'm glad God allowed him to live. I pray that people (throughout the world) who are mentally incapable, disabled, or those with special needs will be treated with love, dignity, and respect. Also, I pray God's grace, mercy, and strength to those who care for individuals with special needs.

God has a purpose and plan for every human being on the face of the earth, whether God's purpose and plan makes sense to us or not. And though it's human for us to question or even struggle with our human experience and why God allows certain things to take place, we fare better when we yield to God's infinite wisdom and control as opposed to trusting our finite understanding of things. After Chester's death, it was six years until I was off to Tennessee again to bury a loved one. In 2001, my sister-in-law passed away. Two years later, I would go back to say good-bye to my last brother.

RONNIE

For years after Chester died, Ronnie would always say, "It's just you and me now." Although we were relatively close before the death of our family members, we grew closer together when it was just the two of us. In Ronnie's hometown, he was called "Maestro"; and as I mentioned earlier, he seemed to know everybody. In fact, in the early days when I was a kid, Ronnie had a peculiar relationship with some of his friends.

If my brother happened to be in the neighborhood and saw one of his friends, they would "play the dozens" (talk about each other's mother) or start "cracking on" (joking about) each other. I remember the time my brother and I were going somewhere when we saw one of his friends. Immediately, my brother had to tell him to hold back on playing the dozens because he had his little brother with him, which often surprised people that he had a little brother. Of course, there were peculiar aspects about our relationship as well. The most glaring one is what I call "never shaking the younger/little brother tag." Certainly, the "I'm the older brother" reminders were a given when I was a kid. And, yes, he was old enough to be my father (a young father, mind you). But even in my adult years after I was married with a child, served my country, and was an ordained minister, I was still "the younger/little brother."

As I write these words, I smile as I recall passionate discussions with Ronnie when his thinking or doing was in question, and he would drop the "big brother" line on me. Sure, I respected my brother and his "eldership," but, I must admit, we had different lifestyles, priorities, and ways of thinking and doing things. This is not to suggest Ronnie was lacking in knowledge or that his potential for succeeding in life was far below mine. Ronnie was savvy, intelligent, and well aware of the issues of our day. He had the emotional wherewithal, people skills, and business mind to go farther in life than I could ever imagine. Still, knowing or having the ability to get from point A to Z, and choosing to take those necessary steps is often the key to success for every human being on the face of the earth.

I contend that to err is human, but to learn from one's mistakes and making better life choices toward growth and maturity is wise. In spite of my vulnerabilities and imperfections, I had given my life to Christ and was striving to incorporate Christian values into my life. This, and this alone, kept me from total self-destruction and choosing to remain on a path that would lead to spiritual death. On the other hand, Ronnie had a set of values and beliefs that influenced his behavior and choices in a more personally gratifying manner in terms of what he practiced in his daily living.

Though Ronnie was kind, caring, personable, and knowledgeable, his "love of the streets" caused much consternation for those of us who loved him. Of course, there are many dangers, toils, and snares lurking in the mist for those who are hypnotized by the lure of the streets. All this notwithstanding, my biggest concern for him (not only myself, but other family members as well) was his inability to see those around him who didn't have his best interests at heart (similar to Maurice). Often, Ronnie trusted the wrong people (mostly those he ran or dealt with). I remember a certain family member confiding in me that she felt his inability to recognize these negative individuals would be his downfall. She had plenty of reason to feel this way. One good example was the time my brother took a fall for a false friend's misdeeds. This so-called friend let my brother take the fall, endure the consequences, and suffer—at least, this was the word on the streets. Deep down inside, my brother knew about all the "trappings" of dealing with questionable people in questionable places. Yet in light of these things, Ronnie failed to remove himself from the vultures and negativity.

Ronnie remained faithful to his own path (a path that seemed to short circuit God's best for his life). As Ronnie got older and his body began to wear down, I wondered how long my brother could keep living life on his terms. Since Ronnie had been overweight for a very long time, I was even more concerned about his overall welfare. Though I'm sure Ronnie slowed down, I don't know if he ever did an about-face. Mainly when we got together, we didn't talk much about his personal affairs—though other family members might hint or express their ideas concerning my brother and his "perceived" activities. Nevertheless, I wasn't stupid. I observed and listened to him and others around him and surmised Ronnie was going to do things his way. I felt this way for a long time until a few things happened to him before his last curtain call on life. The first event happened in 2001.

In 2001, I was stationed at Bolling Air Force Base, DC. I was an active duty chaplain and officer who pastored a congregation on base, provided chaplain support to several units and organizations, and counseled many individuals and families. On the morning of September 11, 2001, I was in my office, when one of the chaplains mentioned that a plane had hit the Twin Towers in New York. At this point, several staff members gathered around the television to view the reports on CNN. Then, we saw another plane hit the other Twin Towers building. We couldn't believe what we were witnessing. It was beyond words. It was all happening so fast. Then, out of nowhere, we felt the chapel shake. We didn't know whether the base had been hit or what. We gathered ourselves together, and soon learned that the Pentagon had been hit.

Once the chapel staff got the marching orders on how to respond to this awful tragedy, we moved forward in providing pastoral care and support to the base, members at the Pentagon, and those affected by this tragedy in the DC region. I remember counseling a woman who lost her husband in this tragedy. She had children and deeply loved her husband. It was a devastating time; yet, it was a time when Americans came together and supported one another. For a long time, chaplains went over to the Pentagon to conduct services; provide ministry; and offer counsel. I'm very grateful God allowed me, the chaplains, and other helping professions to bring healing to those touched by this tragedy. It was an experience I shall never forget. However, in the midst of these events, Ronnie's wife died.

Ronnie and my sister-in-law were married a long time, and her death was unexpected. In fact, she was only in her early fifties. Of course, I was shocked and saddened to learn of her death. I will always remember her as a hardworking woman who loved her family and encouraged her children to make the most of their lives. I knew her death was a blow to my brother; but I never knew how much because Ronnie didn't show or share a lot of emotion. However, a year later (in regard to the second thing that shook my brother) I discovered how much and more.

In 2002, Ronnie had to have a very serious heart procedure and needed surgery. Ronnie's life was at stake. During my brother's stay at the hospital, he talked a lot about putting flowers on my sister-in-law's grave and how much he missed her. Ronnie broke down and cried (the first time in my life I ever saw him cry). In every relationship or marriage, there are joys and sorrows, laughter and sadness, challenges and victories. But witnessing my brother weep for his wife was very moving. It was a very emotional time for him. During a few of his emotional moments, I became a vehicle for him to unleash his feelings. In some way, Ronnie knew this could be the end of the road for him, so he was very expressive leading up to his procedure.

In those days and moments before he would find out if God would be merciful enough to grant him a few more days on the earth, I believe Ronnie contemplated certain aspects of his life. Perhaps, Ronnie's reckoning with his mortality and realization that he needed something more than his way of thinking could be his breakthrough to seeing life from a more spiritual perspective. Or maybe understanding how little control we have over life could awaken his soul to reach out to God's purpose and plan for his life as he's never done before! I do believe something happened to my brother's heart during this fragile time in his life. To what extent, I do not know.

Fortunately, God spared my brother's life. He made it through his procedure, and Ronnie was given more time to live. After Ronnie left the hospital, I know he had to slow down and not be as active as he had been in the past. From time to time, he would mention a physical challenge here or there; but for the most part, he seemed in good spirits. Although I don't remember a lot of conversation about me supporting him through his ordeal, I know he was glad I was there, even though I probably said a few things he didn't want to hear in regard to taking care of himself ("younger/little brother tag in full force").

In looking back, I'm glad I was there because it was just "the two of us" as he would often say. Once we got through his procedure, I thought I'd have my brother around for a long time. I don't know to what extent his involvement continued with his so-called friends, but he told me he had to make some changes in his life. I didn't think God would take my brother anytime soon—knowing that he was the only brother I had left. Yet God had other plans.

In the fall of 2003, I got a call from Ronnie's stepson. He told me Ronnie had a heart attack while driving, pulled over in a lot, and died! I couldn't believe it. Ronnie, my last oldest brother, had been in my life over forty years. Together, we lived through the death of many loved ones. Now, I stood alone—the last member of my immediate family. After talking to Ronnie's stepson, I gathered myself and prepared for my journey back to Tennessee. On my way there, I decided to do something I had never done before. I decided to officiate at my brother's funeral. With God's help, I took care of the service, preached, and laid my brother to rest. I remember when I first saw my brother in his coffin, he looked like he was asleep. He had this peaceful look on his face that let me know God was working on my brother to the end. After my brother's death, four years passed by until I lost my niece—Billy's daughter. Although she had a medical condition most of her life, she was only a few years older than I was! A year later, I retired from the Air Force as an Air Force chaplain in the rank of Major (served 1981–2008). Although relatives and immediate family members were gone, I would never forget them. I had no control over how or when they would leave me. But I do have control over how I celebrate them. "The Way It Is" conveys the reality of my losses. "The Way It Can Be" conveys how God turned my losses into victories!

The Way It Can Be – loss to victory

As I look back over "The Way It Was" and "The Way It Is" chapters of my journey with loss, I'm grateful for God's magnificent ability to work through my circumstances in helping me to become better not bitter; encouraged not discouraged; and hopeful not helpless. God has shown me that I must never limit Him or myself by the negative past or painful experiences. In God, I'm victorious and more than a conqueror. This is my testimony pertaining to "The Way It Can Be" for anyone willing to embrace God, our Creator, and His Son, Jesus Christ. In light of this fact, my journey has helped me to grow in three crucial areas: Faith, Service, and Life.

GROWING IN FAITH

I wish I could tell the world that once I acknowledged and embraced God through Jesus Christ, my world was perfect, but it wasn't. I wish I could say once I accepted the Lord I didn't have any more problems, and all my life questions were logically answered, but that didn't happen. I wish I could say I became a perfect person and never made any mistakes or experienced struggles in life after accepting the Savior, but I can't! And if most flawed, imperfect, limited believers living in a flawed, imperfect world were truthful and honest, I believe they would say the same. I've learned over the years that achieving human perfection or striving to reach unattainable, unrealistic goals should never be one's aim. Rather, the perfect situation for humanity is this: to grow in faith and in one's relationship with God. When this happens, maturity and change can take place. Therefore, I can personally verify that my belief system, values, perspective, outlook, and attitude have been positively influenced by a growing faith and relationship with God. So when it comes to dealing with loss and life, one's belief system, values, perspective, outlook, and attitude play a major role in how one lives and copes with loss.

How important is one's belief system as it pertains to life? Primarily, one's belief system is important because it directly influences how one thinks, feels, and behaves. Often, we live out our beliefs, and our beliefs dictate how we understand, process, and experience life. Still, how a person comes to believe what he or she believes is the ultimate question to be realized. Throughout most of my (ministerial) life, I've come across people searching for truth and answers about God, humanity, life, and the afterlife. Since there are so many religions and belief systems and so many points of view concerning these issues in our world, people come away with different conclusions. For some, there is no God; no heaven or hell; no consequences for things done on earth beyond this life; and no hope beyond our five senses. For others, some believe there may be a God, but one can't intimately know Him; or God (Higher Power) is disinterested in human affairs; or if one lives a moral life (according to one's own standards), one will make it to a better place in the afterlife; or all paths lead to the same destiny. Others embrace belief systems that advocate one working his or her way to God or heaven; or if one doesn't go through this life successfully, he or she will have an opportunity to do it again via reincarnation; or a person can attain a state of consciousness by which he or she mentally transforms into a state of bliss. Still, I know people who have given up their search for truth to solely exist or live life on their own terms—dismissing a need to search for any truth beyond their own opinions.

Since I did not create the order of life and death, the world, or myself, it would seem unnatural for me to create my own truth. How can any limited, flawed human being dare do this? However, to me it's natural to search for truth because God created humanity with a hunger for truth—His truth. Whether you want to acknowledge or embrace the Creator, God has reserved a special place in the human heart that only He can fill. Thus, our relationship and response to our Creator and His will is the most important issue relevant to our existence both in this life and the life to come.

In my estimation, it's our relationship and response to our Creator that shapes our belief system and understanding of things pertaining to life, death, and afterlife. I believe the Bible most truthfully and supremely addresses our condition and need for redemption and salvation like none other. Clearly, the Bible spells out how our fellowship with God was compromised and broken through Adam and Eve's rebellious, self-serving acts. In terms of our position in life, we're lost, sinners by nature, and condemned to judgment and punishment apart from God's intervention. Therefore, according to God's word, our relationship and fellowship with God needed to be restored.

St. John 3:16–18 says, "For God so loved the world that He gave His only begotten Son, that whoever believes in Him should not perish but have everlasting life. For God did not send His Son into the world to condemn the world, but that the world through Him might be saved. He who believes in Him is not condemned; but he who does not believe is condemned already, because he has not believed in the name of the only begotten Son of God." These truths resonate and bear witness to my soul. In no other belief system or doctrine is my condition diagnosed and the antidote supernaturally provided. In no other belief system are the forces of evil; the impact of sin and selfishness; the contradictions and the distractions of secular culture; and God's grace, mercy, love, and power more clearly displayed than in God's Word.

No other entities can say they left their heavenly throne; took the form of humanity; suffered, bled, died, and arose again for my (humanity's) salvation except God, through Jesus. Not only does God through Jesus restore you unto salvation, God restores the weak, fallen Christian that becomes unfocused or deceived by the devil's trickery. And, God restores one who has become a casualty of temptation and the pressures of life. In-spite of it all, my evolving faith and belief in God has helped me navigate through personal losses and the storms of life.

God may not take away the possibility of losing someone near and dear to our hearts. If we must deal with this experience, He can give us the strength to overcome the pain. I'm convinced that God has positively influenced my behavior beyond my willpower, strength, or ingenuity, and He has given me the wherewithal to keep moving forward. As I consider how my growing faith has influenced my belief system, I'm equally appreciative in how it's influenced my values or value system.

The million-dollar question, in reference to your values or value system is, "What do you deem most important or worthy? Perhaps, a good follow-up question to this is, why do you value what you value, and to what degree do you value it? This subject reminds me of the story in the Bible about the young, rich ruler who came to Jesus, and asked him about attaining eternal life. "Now a certain ruler asked Him, saying, "Good Teacher, what shall I do to inherit eternal life?" So Jesus said to him, "Why do you call me good? No one is good but One, that is God. You know the commandments: 'Do not commit adultery,' 'Do not murder,' 'Do not steal,' 'Do not bear false witness,' 'Honor your father and your mother.'" And he said, "All these things I have kept from my youth." So when Jesus heard these things, He said to him, "You still lack one thing. Sell all that you have and distribute to the poor, and you will have treasure in heaven; and come, follow Me." But when he heard this, he became very sorrowful, for he was very rich. And when Jesus saw that he became very sorrowful, He said, "How hard it is for those who have riches to enter the kingdom of God! For it is easier for a camel to go through the eye of a needle than for a rich man to enter the kingdom of God" (St. Luke 18:18–25).

In dissecting this story as it relates to values, it is clear that the young, rich ruler valued at least three things: eternal life, religion, and riches. On the surface, this guy seemed like a pretty decent, conscientious, devoted individual. He sought out the right person able to answer the right question pertaining to the afterlife. He articulated piety and devotion in following religious values. Although he might have inherited his fortune, I believe his wealth indicated that he was a diligent, hardworking, business-minded man. However, by his own admission, his initial concern was in regard to inheriting eternal life. He seemed to place a great amount of value and worth on obtaining eternal life. And when Jesus asked him about keeping the Commandments, he seemed pretty confident about his religious fidelity.

But Jesus' words to him in selling all he had and distributing it to the poor revealed something else about his value system and the value he placed on eternal life. Was inheriting eternal life really important to him? I believe it was, but how important was it to him? Intellectually, he must have known that he can't take it with him, or enjoy his riches beyond this life! Intellectually, he must have known that whatever he accumulated on earth (in terms of material things) will one day perish. Intellectually, he had to know that following the one who could answer his questions and promise him an everlasting treasure in heaven was far better than anything he could attain on earth. However, emotionally, he valued his riches and position in life more than eternal life and treasures in heaven! Jesus didn't need the young, rich ruler's money; but He wanted to reveal where the young man's heart and devotion resided —what he valued most.

The young man walked away "feeling" sorrowful because he sided with his emotions instead of embracing what was right and true—a truth beyond this world. If the truth were told, I think we all have some of the young, rich ruler's tendencies in us. We know that this life is temporal, and we want something greater. But we struggle in letting go of the finite because our values (what's important to us) are limited to this world.

Throughout my life and journey with loss, God has helped me define my values/value system. I value my family, friends, and life. But I highly value my relationship with God. Does that mean it's always easy to separate from the emotional tie I have to family, friends, possessions, and life from what's spiritually and eternally beneficial? Not really. As I mentioned earlier, human beings are flawed and imperfect. We tend to get attached to people, places, things, and it's hard to see life beyond these things. However, God can help you to think and live life on another level. The more I live, the more I discover I'm much better off when I put my relationship with God before any other relationship and when I put God's Word, purpose, and plan for my life before anything else.

Depending on what it is or the sacrifice, it can be a struggle to let go or align yourself with God's direction. But I've always been better for it. Like the young, rich ruler, sometimes we feel like we're giving up too much to inherit eternal life or follow Jesus. Intellectually, we know that nothing on earth lasts forever. Individuals change. Relationships change. Life changes. Yet we know when we leave this earth (and all of us will leave it at some point), we cannot take anything with us. Therefore, I must remind myself that the condition of my soul and living according to God's values trumps anything I can gain in this world. Faith in God's word helps you to stay focused on the right values and can shape your perspective on life as well. If your belief system is what you believe to be true and your values are most important to you, then your perspective is how you see, understand, and process things.

When you've lost everyone in your immediate family, plus other significant loved ones, it can be a challenge to maintain a healthy, positive perspective concerning life. A few years ago, I remember talking to an individual who had lost several family members. Several times during our conversation, he expressed how difficult this was for him. This guy was so depressed and discouraged he told me that if he lost another loved one, he would kill himself. I could relate to his mental and emotional pain of losing loved ones, though I never felt like killing myself. However, I offered him a different perspective of looking at his situation (not limiting himself to negative thinking, but gaining a perspective beyond the loneliness, fear, doubt, worry, anger, pain, and disappointment of losing these individuals in his life).

First, and foremost, I asked him to consider taking his feelings, cares, and frustrations to God. Although he had a church background, knew Scripture, and acknowledged some positive results in turning to God in his past, he began to focus more on his losses than on God's ability to bring hope, healing, and meaning to his life. His perspective had become one of focusing on the negative: "I've lost everybody." "Why do bad things always seem to happen to me?" And "I refuse to be victimized anymore" (in terms of losing any more family members or significant loved ones in his life). As we processed some of these feelings, I tried to help him discover how he could see life from a more spiritual, positive perspective instead of allowing events or circumstances to distort one's total view of self and life.

Is losing loved ones hard, devastating, or overwhelming? In many cases it can be. It was certainly those things and more when I lost my mother. And it was terribly difficult when he lost his loved ones. What if one went to God and asked our Creator for healing and help in the matter? What if God (in time) helped one to look at lost loved ones more as a gift that keeps on giving through memories and in celebration of their lives instead of feeling they're gone and that's it.

There's no time limit on the grieving process. It may take one person a certain amount of time before he or she can accept the loss and move forward and another person more or less time to do the same. Having God in the picture brings a supernatural element into play that you can't generate on your own. If I go back to the young man who shared his feelings and perspective concerning his losses and add a different (more spiritual) perspective as an example, I believe the results will be crystal clear.

When I began to take some of his statements and reflect them back to him, he discovered how untrue and defeating they could be. When he expressed, "I've lost everybody," was this really true? Of course, he felt like it was true. When he described how close and connected he was to certain individuals who passed away, it was understandable that he would feel like everybody was gone. However, his statement and feelings were inaccurate. In fact, he had children and other relatives in his life who loved him very much and needed him. By feeding his "I've lost everybody" mental and emotional perspective, he was unable to allow his departed loved ones to inspire his life, and he was unable to embrace the love of his family and friends.

The same can be said concerning his statements about "Why do bad things always seem to happen to me" and "I refuse to be victimized anymore." When you're under the weight of adversity, pain, or suffering, it's natural to magnify the situation to the extent that nothing seems right about life. Equally true, when one has suffered much loss, it's conceivable to "feel" as though "I've taken enough, and I'm not taking anymore." As I listened to this individual list the bad things that had happened to him and why he had enough, I got to a point in the conversation when I asked about some positive things that occurred in his life.

After some deliberation and determination to stay with the painful events in his life, he began to reflect on some positive things. He talked about the love and support of family; attaining an education; being gifted with talents and skills he's used in the church; bad things that could have happened in his life, but didn't; situations where he found favor; and a God who loved him more than he could imagine. So, even though he felt like bad things always happened to him, this wasn't true. Intellectually, he clearly acknowledged this fact. But emotionally, it was hard not to "feel" like every time he turned around something bad was happening to him or he wasn't going to take anything else of this magnitude. What helped him gain a better perspective of his situation and future (whether he would experience pain again) was believing in a God who loves us and who can help us through adversity and loss instead of staying stuck in adversity and loss.

In the book of Job, Job went through a period in his life in which he experienced some catastrophic events. Initially, he dealt with these challenges in a spiritual, non-emotional way. In other words, Job's faith in God seemed to influence his perspective and how he responded to these calamities. However, the weight of these realities caused him to buckle emotionally until he reverted back to exercising his faith in God's perspective of things—which redirected his perspective. Observe parts of his story.

> Now there was a day when his sons and daughters were eating and drinking wine in their oldest brother's house; and a messenger came to Job and said, "The oxen were plowing and donkeys feeding beside them, when the Sabeans raided them and took them away— indeed they killed the servants with the edge of the sword; and I alone have escaped to tell you!" While he was still speaking, another also came and said, "The fire of God fell from heaven and burned up the sheep and the servants, and consumed them; and I alone have escaped to tell you!" While he was still speaking, another also came and said, "The Chaldeans formed three bands, raided the camels and took them away, yes, and killed the servants with the edge of the sword; and I alone have escaped to tell you!" While he was still speaking, another also came and said, "Your sons and daughters were eating and drinking wine in their oldest brother's house, and suddenly a great wind came from across the wilderness and struck the four corners of the house, and it fell on the young people, and they are dead; and I alone have escaped to tell you!" Then Job arose, tore his robe, and shaved his head; and fell to the ground and worshipped. And he said, "Naked I came from my mother's womb, and naked shall I return there. The Lord gave, and the Lord has taken away; Blessed be the name of the Lord." In all this Job did not sin nor charge God wrong." (Job 1:13–22)

After Job received the first wave of bad news, Job held to his spiritual convictions. Next, Job was afflicted with painful boils all over his body. Then Job's wife told him (in response to his situation) to curse God and die. Then, three of Job's friends came and sat with him for a week to support him during this ordeal. Eventually, they would blame Job for his calamities. It was at this time, you could see the weight of these calamities on Job's spirit. Soon, Job would utter these words:

> "May the day perish on which I was born, and the night in which it was said, 'A male child is conceived.' May that day be darkness; May God above not seek it, Nor the light shine upon it. May darkness and the shadow of death claim it; As for that night, may darkness seize it; May it not rejoice among the days of the year, May it not come into the number of the months. Oh, may that night be barren! May no joyful shout come into it! May those curse it who curse the day, those who are ready to arouse Leviathan. May the stars of its morning be dark; May it look for light, but have none, And not see the dawning of the day; Because it did not shut the doors of my mother's womb, Nor hide sorrow from my eyes. Why did I not die at birth? Why did I not perish when I came from the womb? Why did the knees receive me? Or why the breasts, that I should nurse? For now I would have lain still and been quiet, I would have been asleep; Then I would have been at rest with kings and counselors of the earth, who built ruins for themselves, Or princes who had gold, who filled their houses with silver; Or why was I not hidden like a stillborn child, like infants who never saw light? There the wicked cease from troubling, and there the weary are at rest." (Job 3:3–17)

Job never said the words, "Bad things always happen to me" or "I will never be victimized again." But it's clear that at some point when the realities of his predicament flooded his soul, his perspective went from "naked I came into the world, naked I will leave it, blessed be the name of the Lord" to "curse the day I was born." I'm not sure if he was clinically depressed or consumed with grief, but his focus changed the more he internalized his losses instead of focusing on his spiritual convictions concerning God's sovereignty and the mindset to be grateful and praise God in all situations! As previously mentioned, it's often easier to acknowledge truth ("naked I come into the world") than to allow this truth to keep us emotionally sound as we deal with loss/adversity/calamity ("curse the day I was born").

When Job brought his questions and concerns about his situation to God, God asked him questions about life, creation, the universe, and so on. Through his dialogue with God, Job realized his finite understanding; his inability to see the "big picture"; and that his limited power was inferior to God. Eventually, Job opened himself up to a sovereign God who is always in control and able to provide meaning and purpose to our lives, even when things seem out of control. Job was able to readjust his perspective and not see himself or his plight in the same way. Hear Job's words to God:

> "I know that you can do everything. And that no purpose of Yours can be withheld from You. You asked, 'Who is this who hides counsel without knowledge?' Therefore I have uttered what I did not understand, Things too wonderful for me, which I did not know. Listen, please, and let me speak; You said, 'I will question you, and you shall answer me.' I have heard of You by the hearing of the ear, But now my eye sees You. Therefore I abhor myself, and repent in dust and ashes." (Job 42:2–6)

It took Job some time to gain a better perspective in dealing with pain and suffering. It took the individual I talked to time to gain a healthier perspective about his life (although I sense that he continued to struggle to some degree). And it has taken much time for me to grow in faith and allow God to influence my perspective regarding my challenges and losses. Were my beliefs, values, and perspective tested and stretched by loss and suffering? Sure. But I've discovered that God is able to unlock His wisdom, love, and power in influencing my life in profound ways. If I had never experienced loss, I would not know and appreciate what it means to be victorious in life. Someone once said, "In order to be a victor, one must overcome or defeat something." God gave Job the victory over his struggles, and He's done the same for me. Not only does God give us victory as He changes our beliefs, values, and perspective, He can help us to be victorious concerning our outlook and attitude.

When I think about the words "outlook" and "attitude," I think about how internal and external views affect one's frame of mind and behavior. Depending upon where I am in life or what I base my life on, my outlook (or when I survey or evaluate my life) can be optimistic or pessimistic. In the same fashion, depending upon how I process life, events, and circumstances, my attitude and how I respond to life may be positive or negative. Two good examples of this are a conversation I had with a woman dealing with fear and family issues and the biblical story of two men traveling on a road from Jerusalem to a village called Emmaus.

Less than a year ago, I had a conversation with a woman who had attempted suicide because she was very distraught about her situation. She had a hurtful past, had experienced a painful divorce, and was having trouble connecting with one of her children. Aside from her painful past and divorce, her relationship with her teenage son really negatively affected her outlook and attitude. Somehow, her relationship with her son had become strained over the last year or so, and she couldn't seem to make it better. These things began to overwhelm her, and she couldn't seem to get things back on track.

In her mind, she couldn't fix the fact that her marriage failed and this impacted her children (some more than others); she couldn't fix the struggles parents and teenagers have with each other when kids think they know more than parents (or at least when kids feel they know better than their parents concerning their lives); and she couldn't seem to fix her expectations in relation to how she felt her child should respond to her. She could not envision a life without the total affection or presence of her child. In fact, her words to me are paraphrases as, *If something happened to my child or if my child won't love me, I don't want to live.*

Her outlook and attitude was linked to something she could not control—the love of her son. Therefore, her happiness, future success, self-worth, meaning, and purpose in life seemed to all hinge on this relationship! Most people on the outside looking in might say, "How could she allow her relationship with her son define who she is, her happiness, peace of mind, and future?" As we talked, I tried to help her to see how unfair it was to give anyone that kind of power and control over her life. To a point, she agreed it wasn't healthy.

Emotionally, her identification, affirmation, and life were so interwoven with her teenager that she could not separate her "feelings" from the truth—creation's relationship with its Creator must trump creation's relationship with creation. Her outlook and attitude was, if I can't have the type of relationship with my son that I want or if my son is not in my life, I would rather be dead! The fear of losing her child, the trepidation of dealing with unmet expectations and needs in regard to someone important in her life, and assuming the rest of her life would be unlivable without a loving relationship with this person caused her to almost end her life.

What if her outlook and attitude was God loves me, and I'm going to put my life and my relationships in His hands? Or, He can forgive, heal, and restore me, and I refuse to give anyone or anything power over my life besides God. Or, my life and God's purpose and plan for me are bigger than any relationship or loss I may experience. Also, what would happen if she were to say to herself, I know my divorce may have had a negative impact on my children, but I'm going to take care of myself; set healthy boundaries with my children; and love and support my children the best I can, with God's help? This is a different outlook and attitude concerning loss, unmet expectations, and life. No, I can't control everything in life, and people aren't going to always do what I want them to do no matter what I do or how hard I try. I can, however, control what I can control and trust God with the rest. Actually, I can trust God with it all because what may seem too hard for me is never too hard for God! God can help one have a healthy, positive outlook and attitude about self, relationships, and life.

Another example of how your outlook and attitude influences your life is the story of two men traveling to Emmaus after the death and burial of Christ and subsequent Resurrection. In setting the stage for this story, Jesus had been dead and buried for three days, and for many who followed and looked forward to Jesus redeeming Israel, it was a sad time. However, when Mary Magdalene, Joanna, and Mary went to Jesus's tomb, His stone had been rolled away. As the women tried to figure out what had happened, two angels appeared to them and reminded them that Jesus had said He would be crucified and rise again on the third day. As they accepted these words, they went and told these things to the eleven remaining disciples and others in their company. Next, the Scripture shifts to two men traveling to Emmaus who had been with the disciples when the women told them about Jesus. While traveling, two things took place. They contemplated Jesus's

crucifixion and the things the women shared with them; and Jesus came
and walked with them (though they didn't recognize Him at the time).
Still not quite convinced of Jesus's Resurrection, the two men's outlook
and attitude seemed bleak and hopeless until they later realized Jesus
had risen and walked with them to Emmaus. Observe a portion of this
story in St. Luke 24:13–25, 31–32.

"Now behold, two of them were traveling that same day to
a village called Emmaus, which was seven miles from Jerusalem.
And they talked together of all these things which had happened.
So, it was, while they conversed and reasoned, that Jesus Himself
drew near and went with them. But their eyes were restrained, so
that they did not know Him. And He said to them, "What kind
of conversation is this that you have with one another as you walk
and are sad?" Then, Cleopas answered and said to Him, "Are You
the only stranger in Jerusalem, and have You not known the things
which happened there in these days?" And He said to them, "What
things?" So they said to Him, "The things concerning Jesus of
Nazareth, who was a Prophet mighty in deed and word before God
and all the people, and how the chief priest and our rulers delivered
Him to be condemned to death, and crucified Him.

"But, we were hoping that it was He who was going to redeem
Israel. Indeed, besides all this, today is the third day since these
things happened. "Yes, and certain women of our company, who
arrived at the tomb early, astonished us. When they did not find
His body, they came saying that they had also seen a vision of
angels who said He was alive. And, certain of those who were with
us went to the tomb and found it just as the women had said; but
Him they did not see." Then He said to them, "O foolish ones, and
slow of heart to believe in all that the prophets have spoken!"

After Jesus walked with them, expounded upon the Scriptures and things concerning Him, and broke bread with them, they realized Jesus was alive. The Bible says, "Then their eyes were opened and they knew Him; and He vanished from their sight. And they said to one another, "Did not our hearts burn within us while He talked with us on the road, and while He opened the Scriptures to us?"

During Jesus' ministry on earth, He talked about His mission, purpose, and resurrection; but when He was crucified, people seemed to have forgotten His truth. Judging by their five senses instead of their faith, most believers (including the two men in this story) were discouraged and defeated. People felt the loss and death of Jesus equaled the loss and death of His promises and their future. And in the case of the two men walking to Emmaus, they were still discouraged in spite of the fact Jesus was walking by their side.

Again, it's fascinating how quickly we can abandon truth and positivity and cling to our limited understanding of things and negativity. It was only after their eyes were opened and they reflected upon Jesus expounding the truth to them that their outlook and attitude changed. Most of us are not much different than the two men in this story. We have expectations, hopes, and dreams concerning how we want things to work out. When there seems to be some deviation, change, or challenge to our hopes, we struggle. Yet, when our faith is rooted and grounded in who God is; His great love for us; and His ability to enable us to fulfill His purpose and plan for our lives and navigate us through the challenges of life, we're able to be hopeful, move forward, and live a confident, victorious life! These are the things I've learned as I've grown in faith in my journey with loss. In addition to growing in faith, I've grown in service and life.

GROWING IN SERVICE

Often when I've talked to people about their calling or purpose in life, people tend to think of a job, position, or certain title. I believe God has given humanity the same purpose, but we carry it out in different ways. So what's humanity's purpose? Serve God and one another. In other words, I can't be all that I can be unless I serve the One who created me and is responsible for my life. As I love and serve my Creator and Lord Jesus Christ, I fulfill His plan and purpose through obedience to His will, loving and respecting myself, and loving, respecting, and serving others. Thus, my journey with loss has helped me to understand and see the significance of service. As a result, I've learned at least two things pertaining to loss and service: the world doesn't revolve around me (or anyone); and God chooses how He prepares one for service.

When I was growing up, one of my father's favorite sayings to me was "Son, things are tough all over." Normally, Dad would offer these words when I was dealing with something negative or when life didn't seem to fit my aspirations or expectations. In essence, Dad wasn't advocating that I discount or minimize what I was dealing with. He was advocating I put my situation in the context that I'm not the only one who deals with adversity or life's challenges. Life can be tough for everyone!

No one is exempt from loss, difficulties, and problems. Yet, it's easy to focus on one's negative circumstances or issues and not put things into perspective. I don't know how many people have actually done this, but I've been guilty of "the world revolves around me" syndrome. Not intentionally or in an arrogant way, I've done so by allowing the "Woe is me" syndrome to linger on the edges of my soul and fight against the promise of hope, affirmation, and fulfillment I've discovered in God's word. There have been times in my life when I've had to stop myself from rehearsing the pain, unmet expectations, or hurts of the past. I've had to denounce the idea that certain people (religious, godly, moral, caring, etc.) are exempt from experiencing painful, unfair, or undesirable things. In doing so, I've gained a more balanced perspective on struggle and suffering, and I've been able to help myself and others steer away from self-pity and apathy. Still, one must always stay on guard and fight against negative feelings. It happens to the best of us. Consider the prophet Elijah's attitude and perspective when Jezebel threatened to kill him after God used him to upstage and kill the prophets of Baal.

And (King) Ahab told Jezebel all that Elijah had done, also how he had executed all the prophets with the sword. Then Jezebel sent a messenger to Elijah, saying, "So let the gods do to me, and more also, if I do not make your life as the life of one of them by tomorrow about this time." And when he saw that, he arose and ran for his life, and went to Beer-sheba, which belongs to Judah, and left his servant there. But he himself went a day's journey into the wilderness, and came and sat down under a broom tree. And he prayed that he might die, and said, "It is enough! Now, Lord, take my life, for I am no better than my fathers!" (I Kings 19:1–4)

God had just used Elijah in performing a great miracle (read I Kings, chapter 18), which confirmed to everyone that he was a powerful prophet of the only true God. Though Jezebel had been successful in eliminating some of his fellow prophets, God's favor upon Elijah's life and his important service as a mighty prophet should have given him the courage and strength to deal with Jezebel's threats. However, Elijah became intimidated and a victim of the "world revolves around me" syndrome. He was consumed with fear and despair. Fortunately, Elijah took his situation to God and was able to recover emotionally and spiritually. As I'm sure Elijah grew in relationship with God and service from this experience, I've grown in these areas as well. However, not only has growing in service helped me understand the world doesn't revolve around me, it has helped me understand how God chooses to prepare one for service.

Normally, when you contemplate what job or career path to pursue, you consider the education, training, and experience that will best equip you to be successful in the chosen field. Being an advocate of education and training, I value what academic programs have to offer. However when it comes to serving God and others, no one prepares an individual better than God. Sometimes when you experience loss, pain, or suffering, it's difficult to see how that experience might later benefit your life and how you relate to others. Yet, God knows how to "turn lemons in life into lemonade" and your "midnight into day." Nothing is wasted when we put our lives in the hands of God—not even our mistakes, disappointments, hurts, and sorrows.

Since life is so unpredictable, it's easy to wonder what's going on when life throws you a curveball, as in the case of suffering or loss. Certainly during some of the rough places in my life, I've wondered what was going on or how I could ever benefit from this situation. In other words, how could going through the death of my mom at seventeen years old or Dad dying from cancer when I was twenty-two years old or helping Billy and his friend wash Maurice's blood off the walls of our home (less than two months after the death of my dad) add any value to my life? Standing on their own merits, these tremendous losses would not be desirable or beneficial. However since God has called humanity to serve and called me in particular to minister to others, God has used these experiences in helping me to become more compassionate and empathetic. Let me expound upon this as it relates to ministry.

There's an old saying that aptly demonstrates the value of being compassionate to others, which goes like this, "People don't care how much you know, people want to know how much you care!" As a result of dealing with disappointment, pain, suffering, and loss, I've grown more sensitive to and concerned with the plight of others. Throughout my ministerial life and walking with others dealing with painful events, I've been able to connect, encourage, and provide hope in ways I would not have been able to do without God taking me through some painful experiences. Whereas, I could name many examples pertaining to how my journey with loss has helped me reach out and support others, three particular situations come to mind.

The first situation happened when I was a chaplain in training at a civilian hospital. On this particular day, I had the additional duty of on-call chaplain to go along with my regular assignments. During my shift, I received an emergency call to provide support to a woman (and later her husband) who delivered a baby that had died. When I went into the woman's room, I remember the woman looking like she was in a state of shock, but aware of her surroundings. Although her husband hadn't arrived yet, staff members comforted her.

I walked up to her, introduced myself, told her why I was there, and offered words of comfort. She was very receptive, but understandably sad and devastated by the loss of her child. Knowing this was a very delicate and emotional time for her, I did more listening and providing a ministry of presence than trying to "fix" her or achieve a certain outcome. I didn't tell her things like "I know how you feel"; "I understand what you're going through"; or "you'll be all right." Sometimes, people say these things because they either don't know what to say or think they "should" say something to "fix" the person who's hurting. I didn't try to get her to compartmentalize her feelings or lure her into spiritualizing the situation. I tried to meet her with compassion, support, and walk with her toward hope and healing.

I didn't say superficial or surface things to her because I know from experience they don't work! Can you imagine losing a child and someone coming to you saying, "I know how you feel?" Or "I understand what you're going through?" Of course, one of the most natural responses to these assumptions would be, *Really?* Because unless you have crawled inside a person and can experience exactly what he or she is feeling at that particular time, there's no way of knowing or understanding what a person is going through (even if a person has gone through something similar).

Everybody handles things differently, and it's presumptuous to think you would know exactly how another human being might process a given situation (especially in dealing with loss). Nevertheless, you can be compassionate and thoughtful. You can ask the question, "How would I want to be talked to or cared for if I had lost a child?" Would I want someone who was attentive, thoughtful, and caring or would I want someone who was more interested in "fixing" me or trying to get me to feel what they want me to feel? I kept these things in mind when I ministered to this woman, and her family and friends—when they arrived. After spending much time with them, they expressed their appreciation for my support. I didn't know what it meant to carry a baby, with hopes and dreams for their future and see them vanish away. I didn't know what it was like to think about making arrangements to bury a child. Yet God gave me a compassionate heart through my own suffering, and I was able to reach out and help this woman and her family cope with their loss.

The second situation that comes to mind is when I was an active-duty chaplain deployed in Balad, Iraq during the war. In 2006, I was assigned to the Air Force Theater Hospital (AFTH) at Joint Base Balad as the day shift hospital chaplain (we had another chaplain working nights and between the both of us, we mainly covered the hospital 6 days a week, working twelve-hour shifts). Balad, Iraq, is forty miles north of Baghdad; located within the Sunni Triangle; and AFTH was the hospital where most of the wounded and dying military, civilian, and allies were sent for treatment or (in the case of military) transported to Landstuhl, Germany. During my tour to Iraq, this was probably one of the busiest times of the war, and we were constantly receiving personnel through the emergency center into our facility.

On this particular day, a young man (around eighteen or nineteen years old) was brought into our facility as a result of injuries sustained in a roadside bombing—an Improvised Explosive Devise (IED). Although he looked like a sophomore in high school, he was clearly a sharp, young man, dedicated to the military and our country. As I made my way through the room seeing other patients, I came to him, and we began a conversation. After some preliminary talk, he began to discuss what had happened to him and how he was feeling. He told me how he and others sustained injuries during this traumatic event. But it was his thoughts concerning a particular individual (who worked with him and played a major role in his life) that moved me.

He talked about his supervisor who was traveling with him in a convoy of military vehicles and was killed during this unfortunate event. He fondly shared how his supervisor was a mentor, role model, and great family man. He spoke of his supervisor's wife and children and how sorry he felt for them. Then he looked at me with a very concerned, serious look on his face, and asked, "Chaplain, where do you think he's at?" He went on to say, "I don't believe he went to church a whole lot, he didn't talk much about his religion, and I know he went out sometimes. But he was a good man. Do you think he went to Heaven?"

As I listened to him talk, it was apparent how much he cared for, respected, and appreciated his supervisor. His question came out of a genuine concern for his boss's finality and of needing closure. Because I have wrestled with similar questions from my journey, I shared thoughts with him concerning putting his supervisor in the hands of a loving, wise, just God; continuing to love, honor, and celebrate him in memory; and allowing his legacy to continue through him (as well as his family). Through our discussion, we acknowledged things within our control (personal and life choices, such as living for God) and things out of our control (personal and life choices others make apart from us). We agreed it's always better to be grateful and embrace what a lost loved one meant to us and how we can learn something from his or her life that would help us to be better people, as opposed to trying to determine someone's outcome (especially if a person did not seem very religious or Christian).

Again, there may be some who would say, "As a minister of the Gospel, isn't it your responsibility to evangelize; tell this young man that anyone who isn't a Christian will go to hell, and being a good person alone isn't good enough to make it to Heaven?" My answer to this question would be, "Anyone can smack somebody upside the head with a Bible and preach hell and damnation. However, my journey with loss has taught me that there's a time and place for everything. When a person is in the initial stages of loss, it's not the time to get 'preachy' or enter into a theological discourse. It's a time for listening, caring, and compassion."

Is it too passive or sentimental to embrace a more compassionate approach when people ask if their departed loved one(s) is in heaven?

I don't believe it is. To me, it's about meeting people where they are, providing support, and walking with them toward healing and hope. It's a process, and it takes time. We did talk about the virtues of accepting and living for God and the peace of mind that comes with it. Furthermore, I believed the young man needed to be reached and given hope in how he could move forward before any substantive assessment could be made about his supervisor. In reality, I didn't know what was in his supervisor's heart nor did I know what type of relationship he had with God (though on the surface it may appear he didn't have much of a relationship with God at all).

After much discussion with this young man, I could tell he was beginning to move in a positive direction. It wasn't easy for him to go through this traumatic event that left him injured and mourning the loss of his supervisor, but he discovered he had positive options for how he could move forward. He reaffirmed the power of choice in his own life to choose to live for God and experience the benefits of putting his life in the Lord's hands. He affirmed the power of choice to love and celebrate what his supervisor meant to him. He took major steps in embracing the reality that we can control only what we can control, and what we can't control we must put in God hands.

The third situation that comes to mind took place when I was an active-duty chaplain assigned to a base medical center. One of my units was intensive care, and patients placed on this unit were normally very ill. In regard to this particular case, I started visiting a young man (in his mid-twenties) who was dying. Although initially the young man was so ill he could barely talk, I visited and prayed for him. During the course of several visits, I got a chance to talk with and support his family. However, the person I talked with the most was his mother. His mother was a very kind, positive, Christian woman who loved her son and wanted God to intervene in her son's life in a powerful way.

As I talked with the young man's mother, she would talk about inspirational Scriptures demonstrating God's healing power, and how nothing was too hard or impossible for God to do. In addition, she would ask me to keep praying for her son and agree (according to the Word of God) that her son would be healed. In fact, her very words to me were, "God is going to heal my son, and I know God isn't going to let my son to die." She was very strong in her convictions of how God was going to work this out, and I was strong in my support of her. Although I don't think it's ever a good idea to mandate what God is absolutely going to do, I did not try to put water on her faith or correct her theology. At best, I gently offered thoughts in reference to God's healing and deliverance coming in different ways, and allowing God's will to be done in this young man's life (in hopes to balance or temper things). In terms of God healing her son, my prayer was aligned with this mother—life, healing, and restoration for her son.

In many ways, it was very easy to have compassion and connect with this mother and her son because the situation hit very close to home. Although I would never claim to know what she was going through or understand what she was feeling as a parent praying for a dying son, I did understand her convictions concerning directing one's faith toward God and believing God to turn a desperate situation around as it relates to a family member.

Someone might say, "Why did you allow this woman to get her hopes up high?" "Why would you allow this woman to believe something counter to the direction the young man's situation seemed to be going (death)?" My answer to this would be, "Has not God worked miracles in people's lives before?" "Is it my job to advocate that people reduce God to our circumstances and problems, or is it my job (especially one Christian talking to another) to help one embrace all that God is and what God can do?"

Of course, in embracing all that God is and what He can do, you must always allow God to have the final word! And, His final word may or may not be what you want to hear. Sometimes, God decides to go in a direction different from what we desire. The Bible says, "For My thoughts are not your thoughts, Nor are your ways My ways, says the Lord" (Isaiah 55:8). God sees the big picture and understands things on a level that we can't (again, review the story of Job). So, although God's course of action may not make sense at the time, we must trust that God knows what He's doing. And if you don't know exactly what God's will is for a particular situation, it's far better to be positive and hopeful for a favorable outcome than to accept a verdict before the sentence has been given.

As it turned out, God did take away this young man's suffering and pain. But God did it in His way. The young man passed away. Though the mother was glad her son wasn't suffering anymore and is in a better place, she was praying for a physical healing and deliverance instead of the outcome that took place. As a result of her son's death, one might think the mother's faith would be shattered and she would be devastated. But she wasn't. In fact, she was rather calm (calm as calm can be in this type of situation) and sober when her son passed.

Her actions seemed to say, *I loved my son so much, I was willing to believe against the odds; and even though things didn't turn out the way I wanted, I did my part and I have no regrets.* Also, I remember her saying something similar to "Chaplain, I prayed, you and others prayed, but God had other plans."

Again, I responded to her with compassion. I reassured her that I was there for her and her family; I encouraged her to continue to trust God and allow Him to comfort and strengthen them and to continue to love and celebrate her son's life (as I know she would do regardless of what anyone would say). Although her heart was heavy, she received the support and moved forward.

If being compassionate is a by-product of my journey with loss, I've become more empathetic toward the plight of others as well. Although empathy may have an element of compassion to it, empathy brings another level of service and connection to hurting individuals. I may have sympathy for someone, but that doesn't mean I always identify or see things from that person's perspective. I may care for someone, but it doesn't mean I can shift from my frame of reference and context, and put myself in that person's shoes (as much as humanly possible).

If being compassionate paints a picture of a concerned soul reaching out to someone in an attempt to relieve suffering, being empathetic paints the picture of someone taking on or internalizing an individual's mindset, context (in terms of background, history, and experiences), and feelings to identify and connect with that individual. Since most individuals are well versed in their own frame of reference and context, it's not always easy to empathize with another individual to the point that you can understand why a person would think, feel, or act the way he or she does.

As an example, most people have experienced someone making a remark similar to these: "Well, if it were me, I would have done this or that." Or, "I had the same thing happen to me, and I didn't act that way." However, as I've previously mentioned, the world doesn't revolve around you—especially when providing service to others. It doesn't mean I should abandon or subordinate my beliefs and values in favor of others. Using eyeglasses as an example, it means setting down my glasses and seeing things through someone else's lens (perspective) to see what they're seeing.

So growing in service has definitely helped me highly value empathy because I don't really think you can truly meet a person where he or she is unless you're willing to go where the person is. And if the truth were told, not everyone is willing to go where a hurting person is because (in most cases) it takes a willingness to feel someone's pain and journey with that person to a place of healing and wholeness. As I reflect upon many situations that called for being empathetic in my life, a couple of situations rise to the surface.

Both situations happened when I was a civilian hospital chaplain. The first case involved a health care worker who had attempted suicide because she was fired for stealing and using drugs from her employment. In talking with her, she explained that she started taking medication due to stress and began to abuse it. Because of her position in the hospital, she had access to drugs and could manipulate the system by taking some drugs and covering her tracks. This lasted for several years until she was caught. Of course, she was penalized and fired. Not only did her actions affect whether she would ever work in the health care field again, it affected her family, her self-esteem, and her outlook on life. As a result, she tried to take her life, and if she had succeeded, she would have left innocent loved ones behind who needed her.

Of course, when peers and others learned of her actions and dismissal, not everyone was empathetic. I don't know if anyone was bold enough to express any negative feedback to her face, but she could imagine some of them saying, *She's got to lie in the bed she made* or *She got what was coming to her.* Sure, there's a certain amount of truth to this, but she was well aware that she had blown it. She wasn't in denial about the seriousness of her actions or the negative impact they had on her career, family, and life. She had become so despondent and disappointed in herself that she didn't want to live anymore, in spite of the fact she had people who loved her.

Someone might say, *I could never do anything to myself and leave my children or loved ones behind*, but some folks are in situations in which they feel like, *I've messed up my life so bad, there's nothing I can do to repair it!* People in this situation don't need others piling on and kicking dirt in their faces because they already think and feel defeated. They need some empathy!

When I met with this woman, I listened to her story. I listened to her pain, embarrassment, and self-hatred. I listened to someone who saw no hope or light at the end of the tunnel. So I stepped out of my context and tried to imagine how I would think and feel if I were in her shoes—if I had blown it! Actually, it wasn't that hard because I've made mistakes in my life. Had it not been for the grace of God, I know my life would have been a mess as well! So as I felt her pain, I went (in my mind and heart) where she was and began helping her move beyond the pit of negativity.

I told her, it's understandable to feel broken and discouraged, but there were some important things she needed to consider. First, most people have made decisions and choices in life that they later regret. I said this not to excuse undesirable behavior or unwise decision-making, but to confirm that we are all flawed, imperfect human beings. I reminded her of God's love in spite of our mistakes, and the old adage, "To err is human, to forgive is divine." Sometimes, no matter how badly you think you've messed up, you must turn to the Divine

One (God) and implement the divine antidote (forgiveness) in order to get back on track.

Secondly, it's counterproductive to beat yourself up over past mistakes. I commended her for not making excuses; going into denial; or blaming someone else for the choices she made. She did admit she was wrong. However, I tried to help her see how self-destructive and self-defeating it was to continually beat herself down. I encouraged her by saying that a better alternative when taking responsibility for our actions is to learn from them. If you can learn from your poor choices and mistakes, you can be wiser and more focused while continuing to run the race of life. In addition, spiritually speaking, it takes faith to believe you can rise up after falling down. I can empathize with being knocked down or falling down due to selfishness, yielding to temptation, willfully sinning, etc. And I can even empathize with the feeling of wanting to stay down and not get up because of feeling unworthy. As I communicated to her, as long as you're living and breathing, you should never give up or give in. God has invested too much in us to give up. When we stay down or give up, we short-circuit our lives; become our own judge, jury, and executioner; and dig our own graves!

My third and last overall point to her was to let God have the last word! Since she had a spiritual background and was open to this type of dialogue, I proceeded with the most important truth I could ever offer her. God is our Creator, and Jesus Christ lived, suffered, died, and rose again for humanity's salvation and forgiveness of our sins. Jesus paid the price for our mistakes, blunders, poor choices, and miscues. Does that mean it's all right to live a sloppy, careless, rebellious life? No! It means in spite of our flawed humanity, God has provided a way for us to overcome and be restored! It means God can take our broken lives and make us better, stronger, and wiser. And it means our lives are never over—no matter how bad things may appear—as long as we allow God to intervene and be our lifeline.

During her stay at the hospital, we had many visits where I listened, empathized, and shared those (and other) truths with her. On some days, it seemed like she might take a step back. On other days, she seemed to take some steps forward. By the time she was discharged, she was more hopeful and encouraged than when first admitted. She did come to realize that her life wasn't over, and she had much to live for. She understood that if she were to end her life, she would not only hurt herself, but others as well. Before she left, she thanked me for supporting her. But God helped me to see some things too. More and more, God helps me to see how important it is never to underestimate how God can use one's journey in service to others. As I've mentioned before, with God, nothing we go through is ever wasted. If you stay connected to the Creator, God can use all that you go through in life to work toward a good end.

Another case that called for an empathetic response involved a family who felt their loved one's quality of care was in question, which led to her demise. In this particular scenario, I was a new chaplain on the job and working with other staff chaplains in an attempt to learn my way around the hospital. When another chaplain got a call to visit a dying patient and her family, she wanted me to go with her. Normally, when I visit someone, I immediately go to the floor and talk to the doctor, nurse, or social worker (in some cases two or all three) about the patient and family before I make my visit. Although this chaplain was given some information about the situation, we did check in with a health care provider before visiting the patient and family. I was made aware that the family was upset and somewhat dysfunctional (in terms of relations within their family and how certain members related to staff).

My coworker and I went to the patient's room to visit the patient and her family. The patient was very ill and unable to communicate with us. But she had a good number of family members in her room. Once the dialogue began, there were several family members who voiced their concerns about the situation. Since my coworker got the call, I let her take the lead. She listened and offered support. Soon, she needed to attend another call, so she asked me to stay with the family.

After my coworker left the room, several family members went into more detail about their frustrations. In their estimation, when their family member was admitted to the hospital, she was not admitted with a life-threatening illness. In fact, one of the family members mentioned talking to a staff member and receiving information that she received some medication that she wasn't supposed to receive. As a result, several family members began to believe that the relative had a negative reaction to this medication, causing the patient's condition to take a downward turn. However, certain medical staff members had told the family that the medication in question was not a contributing factor to her current condition; she was sicker than they were aware; and her medical condition had progressively become worse. Also, it was explained to the family that even though her condition was not critical prior to admission, her condition was serious in nature, requiring medical attention.

Regardless of the medical explanations given to the family, some members weren't buying into this. So it created a tense situation. In striving to connect with the family, I asked some family members to talk about their dying loved one. During our conversation, I learned that she was a very caring, Christian woman. I asked a few questions similar to this, "What do you think she would say to you right now?" And "How would she want you to deal with all of this?" Several family members said she would want them to be strong; keep the faith; come together as a family; and know that she's in good hands (in God's hands). By now, additional family had joined the group, and the room was getting a little crowded. Several family members seemed to find some comfort in talking about their dying loved one. In addition to our conversation, someone requested that I pray and read Scriptures. I complied, and this, too, seemed to help.

Unfortunately, their loved one didn't make it, and it was difficult for several family members to take. When one of the family members began to call and notify others about the relative's death, she and others became very emotional. Several blamed the hospital and felt their relative would still be here if mistakes hadn't been made. Others said, "She didn't deserve this"; "We don't have anyone now"; and "Why is she gone?" It goes without saying there was a lot of pain, frustration, despair, and suffering in this room.

Whether some of the family members' convictions were true or false, I do not know. However, I do know, this family needed compassionate, empathetic support. In putting myself in this family's shoes, I tried to step out of my frame of reference into their context. They had just lost the pillar of their family under what many deemed questionable circumstances (I'm not agreeing or disagreeing with them or saying they were right or wrong to feel this way), and this loss was very difficult to accept.

The woman who died was the spiritual center for this family and the moral compass, especially to those who struggled. She constantly encouraged and challenged family members to do the right thing. Now this voice was gone, and several members didn't know what the future held for them. It was not an easy place to find oneself. Although this was a challenging, unique situation, the family and staff appreciated the service I provided.

Someone may ask why this situation was so challenging. It was challenging because, on one hand, the staff was accused of being negligent and contributors to someone's death. On the other hand, a hurting, angry, grieving family had just lost a vital member of its family under a cloud of suspicion. And the chaplain—a part of the staff who works for the organization in question—is trying to comfort the grieving, yet is supposed to remain unbiased and supportive of both family and staff.

As a result of my journey, I could remain empathetic to and supportive of both sides. I knew how it felt to have questions about how medical staff went about their business. I've worked with individuals and family who brought different challenges to the table, and I've lost a pillar in my family. No matter the situation, you can't meet people where they are unless you're willing to go where they are. I was willing to go there, and I was glad I did!

GROWING IN LIFE

I'm very grateful God has transformed my challenges and losses to produce growth in the areas of faith and service. I'm convinced I would not have grown in faith and service if I had not allowed God to turn my losses into victories. Embracing Almighty God, being determined not to stay stuck in a rut, and allowing God to use my journey to serve others has been a major catalyst in moving from "The Way It Is" to "The Way It Can Be." Perhaps the most important reward I've gained from my journey of loss to victory is growing in life—how I live my life. Since I could go on forever in discussing how the Lord has helped me to grow and get better at living my life, I'll highlight three areas that convey my experience the most: God's affirmation versus the negative;

living spiritually versus living carnally; and embracing God's purpose and destiny versus personal ambition.

Regarding God's affirmation versus the negative, several things come to my mind. The first thing that comes to mind is biblical stories. When I reflect upon the Bible, I recall many accounts of how God affirmed and gave people hope in spite of the negative. In fact, if one goes back to Genesis, God put His stamp of approval on humanity from the very beginning and remained true to us, despite of our disloyalty to Him. In looking back at the creation story, we learn that Adam and Eve rebelled against God and were punished and kicked out of the Garden of Eden. Humanity (through Adam and Eve) took on a sinful nature, and our world became flawed and sinful. Even though our rebellion in Adam and Eve had a negative effect, God did not totally abandon us or throw us away. God provided a plan of atonement and restoration, in spite of the punishment. In fact, as one observes the stories from Genesis to Revelation, and how God highly valued a relationship with us, one can see God's overwhelming love, favor, and affirmation toward humanity.

The second thing that comes to mind is internalizing these (biblical) stories. Why is it so important to take heed of God's affirmation through the accounts found in the Bible? It is important because the negative can be very powerful in terms of how it affects self-esteem; hinders how one relates to others; and affects how one deals with life. Where do you find affirmation in an environment full of minefields? How do you navigate through the emotional, psychological, and spiritual storms of life when you experience pain, suffering or loss over and over again? Telling yourself that "Everything will be all right" or "I'm going to use these things to make me stronger" or "I just need to look at the brighter side of life and keep moving down the road" are positive self-talk initiatives that can yield some good results. But I find that positive thinking, positive self-talk, and other human-driven initiatives only go so far. God's affirmation and approval are more sustaining and go deeper than what any man or woman can generate. Life can hit an individual so hard and deep that knowing to think and feel a certain way isn't enough because negativity has a vicious way of discouraging the soul. Knowing this, we need to embrace a spiritual source that's greater than the negative.

The third and last thing that comes to mind is, "Life is a witness." As I've mentioned before, I've witnessed too many times in my ministerial life times when "the negative" has overwhelmed and left individuals hopeless. A person's negative past, poor choices, mistakes, abuse, and so forth have a way of gnawing at one's core to the point where individuals become self-destructive and even question whether life is worth living. Yet, I've witnessed people embrace God and allow Him to begin to put their broken lives back together.

In fact, I recall several individuals who shared horrific stories concerning how their past impacted their lives and how embracing God's affirmation helped bring healing in their lives. In one particular situation, a woman in her middle to later thirties told me that her father "F--- up" her life as a result of him raping her over a number of years when she was a child. She went on to talk about how her self-esteem and sexuality were distorted; how she became very promiscuous and a prostitute; and how she had trouble with the law. As an adult, she had a hard time dealing with the hurt, anger, and pain of the past. In her mind, her father was supposed to love, protect, and guard her from this type of evil. Instead, he was the "monster" that violated and sabotaged her life in the worst way. As hard as it was for her to begin a new path in embracing God's affirmation, the seeds were planted and hope was renewed.

In another scenario, I recall how a woman was so affected by her brother having sex with her when she was a child, she was unable to love and embrace her daughter. At first, it was hard for her to admit out loud that the events with her brother took place because part of her loved her brother. But another part of her was hurt, damaged, and embarrassed that he could do such a thing to her. However, the more she discussed the situation, the painful truth came out. Though she tried to soften the pain in her mind by saying something similar to "He just saw or loved me in a different way," she knew that the boundaries he crossed had a monumental impact on her life. Despite the fact her brother would later harm himself as a result of him realizing the damage he caused her and himself, these events poisoned her soul and caused her to project disdain toward her daughter. During our sessions, it became clear to her that she needed God's affirmation to regain a new, fresh love for herself and daughter. Fortunately, she began allowing God to heal her heart, help her deal with the past, and enable her to establish a more meaningful relationship with her daughter.

In addition to the cases above, I've counseled people who've dealt with debilitating illnesses; addictions; homicidal and suicidal ideations; mental, physical, and emotional issues; and family, relational, employment, and financial challenges as well as loss. I've seen how the negative past and present can become an unbearable weight on one's shoulders. It's understandable that negativity would smack hard against the soul and cause one to buckle. Still, I've discovered that no matter how defeating life may seem or how one thinks and feels, God's affirmation and approval can overshadow the negative. Through embracing God's affirmation by faith through the Biblical stories and Scriptures, you can move beyond the negativity and unpredictable moments in life.

Although life is rarely easy, I can truthfully say, "If it had not been for God on my side and me on His side, I would not have made it. And to this day, I still base my self-worth and future on God's unconditional love, grace, and mercy. When the devil or the individuals he influences bring up the past or hurtful situations to derail or discourage me, I run to God's Word. In fact, I have three favorite Scriptures that depict God's approval and acceptance that help me deal with the past, present, and future. These Scriptures are Romans 8:38–39; Philippians 4:13; and 3:13–14. Hear the spiritual words that have been food for my soul:

> For I am persuaded that neither death nor life, nor angels nor principalities nor powers, nor things present nor things to come, nor height nor depth, nor any other created thing, shall be able to separate us from the love of God which is in Christ Jesus our Lord (Romans 8:38–39).

> I can do all things through Christ who strengthens me (Philippians 4:13).

> Brethren, I do not count myself to have apprehended; but this one thing I do, forgetting those things which are behind and reaching forward to those things which are ahead. I press toward the goal for the prize of the upward call of God in Christ Jesus (Philippians 3:13–14).

So how have these Scriptures impacted my life? In a tremendous way, but let me explain. First, when I internalize the reality that through Christ, nothing can separate me from God's love, it gives me self-worth, confidence, courage, and hope like no other. Because we live in a very challenging, imperfect, and unpredictable world, I need the reassurance that God's love and acceptance of me is greater than anything life throws my way. Not only do I need to know that there's no problem, situation, or circumstance too hard for God, I need to know God won't reject me even if I feel rejected or when people reject me. Through the years, this revelation has allowed me to become more secure in who I am and confident in His great love for me.

Secondly, when I embrace the biblical truth "I can do all things through my Lord and Savior Jesus Christ who gives me strength," I feel empowered and energized. I recognize that not only does God love me, He cares about every aspect of my life. As I journey through life, God is able to give me the strength I need to accomplish what is set before me. In other words, God has equipped me to succeed! Fear, worry, and doubt can no longer take residence in my heart (or in anyone who embraces the truth). And no matter what a particular situation or circumstance calls for, God can give me the strength I need to deal with it appropriately.

Third, when I accept God's truth concerning my limitations, forgetting the past, and pressing forward in Christ in fulfilling my destiny, I feel liberated, approved, and determined to maximize my potential. Not only does God understand my faults, weaknesses, and idiosyncrasies, He encourages me to accept who I am and work toward being the best I can be in Him. In addition, instead of throwing the past up in my face and being unforgiving, God forgives my past and expects me not to allow the past to affect negatively my present and future. As a result, I'm encouraged and strengthened to "press" my way through the storms of life and receive all that God wants me to receive.

The next point of interest (after God's affirmation versus the negative) is "living spiritually versus living carnally." Although the terms *spiritual* and *carnal* signify different things to different people, I'd like to refer to these terms from a perspective I've surmised from the Bible. In this regard, *spiritual* conveys the inward (nonphysical) side of humanity influenced by God/Creator and concerned with one's wellbeing and greater good. *Carnal* or *carnality* conveys the physical or self-gratification side of humanity influenced by the world, one's senses, and one's selfish desires. Therefore, to live a "spiritual" life is to live in harmony and relationship with God our Creator—as God would have one to live in relation to Him, others, the world, and oneself. To live a "carnal" life is to live according to the dictates of one's own will, desires, or culture (world)—over or against being led and influenced by God.

Three things come to mind in regard to "living spiritually versus living carnally": choice, courage, and consequences. First, God has given us a choice in terms of how we live our lives. As I write these words, I can almost hear someone saying, "That's not true! There are many situations and circumstances that cause or influence an individual to live a certain way. For example, what if a person were born poor, despised, disabled, with mental deficiencies, or in a negative environment? What if a person was raised to believe a certain way or experienced negative life-changing events? Don't these things play into the decisions and choices one makes?" They certainly can, but they don't have to.

Life happens to all of us, and pain is real! But we still have choices to make even when we're hurting, challenged, or faced with undesirable situations. This concept is one of the most liberating things I've learned on my spiritual journey and my journey with loss, "I have a choice in how I handle or live through a given situation!" I don't have to automatically be negative or live negatively because I've experienced something negative. I can choose to have a relationship with God and allow God to influence how I relate to Him, to others, to the world, and to myself.

I'm glad God has given us the opportunity to live life on a higher level rather than restricting us to rise no higher than our circumstances or to live according to our flesh (self-gratifying nature). Although living a spiritual life according to God's will requires you to relinquish control over your life and trust God, I've discovered I'm much better off doing things His way instead of my way. In fact, I can't think of one situation in my life where I was impatient or operating out of fear or trying to control a situation, and it worked out better than handling it God's way. I also can't think of one situation where I yielded to temptation, yielded to handling things in a carnal way, or allowed my emotions to override a more spiritual response to the situation and did not regret it. Through the years, I've learned that I'm vulnerable, flawed, and in need of God's help in a great way. In addition, my journey has made me aware of how important it is for me to take responsibility and choose to live a spiritual life over a carnal/self-driven one.

The second point is "courage." It takes courage to make the right decisions in life and live spiritually because it "feels" more natural to live a self-centered life. There's a theme throughout the New Testament that highlights an inward human struggle to do what is spiritual without divine intervention. Romans 7:14–19 captures this struggle best in reference to living according to God's laws and commandments by one's own strength (human nature) when it says,

> For we know that the law is spiritual, but I am carnal, sold under sin. For what I am doing, I do not understand. For what I will to do, that I do not practice: but what I hate, that I do. If, then, I do what I will not to do, I agree with the law that it is good. But now, it is no longer I who do it, but sin that dwells in me. For I know that in me (that is, in my flesh) nothing good dwells; for

to will is present with me, but how to perform what is good that I will to do, I do not do; but the evil I will not to do, that I practice.

Even when one knows it's more beneficial to do the right thing, it seems natural to do the selfish thing. Not only do I know this to be true from situations in my own life, I've talked to many individuals who (regrettably) gave into selfishness instead of yielding to God's way. I remember talking to an individual who didn't really like smoking but wouldn't stop because it took too much effort. The same can be said about a woman I counseled about a negative relationship she was involved in. For starters, she was doing things in the relationship that violated her value and belief system. She also confessed feeling unloved and not respected by her partner. Yet, instead of doing the right thing that would benefit her mentally, emotionally, and spiritually, she continued to stay in an unfulfilling relationship (mainly out of fear, a desire to have a family, and a lack of healthy self-love).

Sometimes, we can continue to live in the flesh or make unwise decisions in life because we fear change; we fear moving out of our comfort zone; or we think we can control what is out of our control. Regardless of the reasons behind our actions, it takes a lot of courage to say "no" to self and "yes" to God. It takes courage to live a spiritual life and trust in God even when you don't see the positive outcome right away. I learned it's better to be courageous and confident that God will never fail us and has our best interests at heart than to yield to fear or selfishness and take steps backwards in life. Fear and carnality work against us. Trusting and being courageous in God work in our favor!

The last point concerning "living spiritually versus living carnally" is "consequences." Perhaps, the greatest motivation to live a spiritual life over a carnal one is living with the consequences of your actions. My spiritual journey and age have helped me to understand and appreciate the value of assessing the consequences of my actions before making a decision. Not that I'm perfect (far from it), but I'm at the point in my life where I want to make good, sound decisions that will positively affect the rest of my days. Often I ask myself, "What's behind this decision?" "Who am I striving to please (myself, others, or God)?" And "How will this decision or action affect my life in the short and long run—does it really matter?"

Individuals who are serious about living the best life possible must ask themselves these types of questions. Sometimes people influenced by society, culture, or self-will handle things differently than someone whose spiritual values and convictions are inspired and influenced by God. As obvious as that may seem, it's easy to sidestep this truth when it comes to consequences. I've heard people say, "I'm grown. I can do what I want," or "I'm going to get mine, no matter what I have to do," or "Most people do it, so there must not be anything wrong with it" to justify their actions. But, at the end of the day, will you take responsibility for your choices and deal with the consequences? Because no matter what others may say or do, we have to deal with the consequences of our choices. If I have to deal with consequences, I'd better think things through.

Along with asking yourself thought-provoking questions and thinking things through regarding dealing with the consequences of living a spiritual versus carnal life, one must take heed of God's word. God's word is the manual for life. When God created humanity, He provided a way for us to know what is acceptable and pleasing to Him, how to live in relationship with one another, and how to live in relationship with Him. Although there are many Scriptures that powerfully convey the results of our decision-making, the following

Scriptures really drive home this point: 1 John 2:15–17, St. Matthew 7:13–14, and St. Matthew 16:24–26.

Do not love the world or the things in the world. If anyone loves the world, the love of the Father is not in him. For all that is in the world—the lust of the flesh, the lust of the eyes, and the pride of life—is not of the Father but is of the world. And the world is passing away, and the lust of it; but he who does the will of God abides forever (1 John 2:15–17).

Enter by the narrow gate; for wide is the gate and broad is the way that leads to destruction, and there are many who go in by it. Because narrow is the gate and difficult is the way which leads to life, and there are few who find it (St. Matthew 7:13–14).

Then Jesus said to His disciples, "If anyone desires to come after Me, let him deny himself, and take up his cross, and follow Me. For whoever desires to save his life will lose it, but whoever loses his life for My sake will find it (St. Matthew 16:24–26).

As much as those Scriptures serve as a sobering wake-up call to be in relationship with God and to live a spiritual life over a selfish, carnal one, Psalm 1:1–3 is very informative and inspirational. Psalm 1 describes who is blessed and who isn't, what things should be avoided and what things should be practiced, and how God's word can transform and cause fruitfulness in life. Thus, Psalm 1 encourages us to experience positive consequences as one embraces God's word.

Blessed is the man who walks not in the counsel of the ungodly, Nor stands in the path of sinners, Nor sits in the seat of the scornful; But his delight is in the law of the Lord, and in His law he meditates day and night. He shall be like a tree planted by the rivers of water, that brings forth its fruit in its season, whose leaf also shall not wither; and whatever he does shall prosper.

Often when thinking of consequences, punishment or penalties enter the mind. But Psalm 1 lets us know we can experience positive results by choosing to live a spiritual life in accordance with God's will. We don't have to remain broken, carnal, or self-centered. God has made a way for us to live life on a higher plane—not as people who don't experience trials, tribulations, or temptations, but as people who choose to daily give God control of their lives to live and experience life as God intended!

So far, I've covered "God's affirmation versus the negative" and "living spiritually versus living carnally" in reference to growing in life as a result of my spiritual journey and journey with loss. The final point is the importance of "embracing His purpose and destiny versus self-ambition." When I think about this subject, I tend to focus on at least two things: success and fulfillment. I focus on success and fulfillment because most people desire and live life in pursuit of these things. Yet, the question that always comes back to mind is, who and what determines whether one has achieved these things?

In determining *who* decides whether one is successful or fulfilled, I'll start with "the human perspective" (apart from God's perspective). In general, mainstream society and modern-day culture applaud people who are self-made; the captains of their own ships; or those who have pulled themselves up by their bootstraps—especially those who were not born with a silver spoon in their mouths.

From childhood to adulthood, our culture supplies us with "rags to riches" stories or "climb the social ladder messages." The sky is the limit for people who work hard and who are determined and self-confident. Those who can overcome barriers and apply themselves can live a fulfilling life. Therefore, in the human perspective, success begins and ends with human initiative and effort. Fulfillment is accomplished through human achievement when elevated in the social, economical, moral (in the self-righteous or cultural sense), and material arenas of life.

So as the "human perspective" proponents might say, "What's wrong with success and fulfillment (understood in this way)? What's wrong with promoting "rags to riches" stories and "climbing the social ladder messages?" "And what's wrong with encouraging people to work hard, be determined, and be self-confident, and overcome barriers? Does everything have to be about God?" Through my spiritual journey and journey with loss, my answer to all of these questions is summed up in two statements, "Leaving God out of the picture limits and undermines the full scope of achieving success and fulfillment." "Since God is our Creator and understands us better than we understand ourselves, we must allow Him to show us what true success and fulfillment are."

Let me further explain. Though there may be some value derived from working hard, being self-determined, and confident, these efforts and achievements are limited to the approval of yourself or others. In others words, I may "feel" good about my standing in life, and others may "pat me on the back" for all the things I've accomplished. However, if I haven't acknowledged and included God in my life or concluded that I could never achieve anything without God's mercy, grace, and favor, my sense of success and fulfillment is shallow. In reference to this, I turn to these Scriptures (Deuteronomy 8:11–18 and St. Matthew 16:26) to illustrate my point. Observe the following Scriptures from the New King James Version:

Beware that you do not forget the Lord your God by not keeping His commandments, His judgments, and His statutes which I command you today, lest—when you have eaten and are full, and have built beautiful houses and dwell in them; and when your herds and your flocks multiply, and your silver and your gold are multiplied, and all that you have multiplied; when your heart is lifted up, and you forget the Lord your God who brought you out of the land of Egypt, from the house of bondage; who led you through that great and terrible wilderness, in which were fiery serpents and scorpions and thirsty land where there was no water; who brought water for you out of the flinty rock; who fed you in the wilderness with manna, which your fathers did not know, that He might humble you and He might test you, to do you good in the end—then you say in your heart, 'My power and the might of my hand have gained me this wealth.' And you shall remember the Lord your God, for it is He who gives you power to get wealth (Deuteronomy 8:11–18).

For what profit is it to a man if he gains the whole world, and loses his own soul? Or what will a man give in exchange for his soul (St. Matthew 16:26)?

In the first set of Scriptures, God is preparing His people for "The Promise Land"—a land promised and ordained for the descendants of Abraham. In essence, He reminds them that they will be given houses, land, livestock, and so forth that they did not attain in their own strength! And God reminds them how He brought them out of the land of bondage, pain, and suffering; fed them while in the wilderness; and brought them to a land of plenty. And lastly, He warns them not to forget where these blessings come from and who gave them power to achieve wealth (prosperity, success, and fulfillment).

In the second set of Scriptures, Jesus challenged those in attendance to think about what it means to "gain the world, but lose your soul." He also asked them what they would exchange or trade for their soul. Jesus called them to look beyond the temporary and limited rewards of this world and consider the condition and fate of their soul. In other words, if a man or woman attains riches, fame, and fortune, but does not attain God and loses his or her soul (forever in hell), would you still consider him or her successful? Or would anyone trade his or her soul for the best this world (apart from God) had to offer? No! Jesus is not saying attaining riches, fame, or fortune is bad in itself. He's saying to be more concerned about your relationship with God and the condition of your soul than being worldly and self-centered. God can provide wealth and prosperity too. But He wants us to keep our priorities straight and have the right perspective about success (God must be first place in our lives, and He will show us how to live abundantly). Therefore, God's words were not only relegated to those people in the Old Testament or those listening to Jesus during His time. God is speaking to all human beings who trust in themselves in attaining success and fulfillment apart from God!

Again, I hear the "human perspective" advocates say, "So you're trying to convince us that when a person achieves something on his or her own (especially those who don't believe in a God), there's some higher power responsible for this, and this higher power must be first in our lives?" Yes, because as the Scriptures clearly point out, God helps us in ways we can't always help ourselves! Had it not been for the mercy and grace of God, I could have been another statistic and an unfortunate victim never realizing my potential and life outside my environment. Had it not been for the mercy and grace of God, I could have remained stuck in negativity after my mother and father died. Had it not been for the grace of God, the times I've become weak, frustrated, and defeated,

I would have given up and thrown in the towel. God deserves to be first because, without Him, we can't do anything!

Nobody has to convince me that life can be overwhelming—life can throw you many fastballs, curveballs, and sliders. And nobody has to convince me that life can become so demanding, out of control, and deflating that it can steal your joy, threaten your sense of hope, and redirect your will to succeed. No, my spiritual journey and journey with loss tell me, "I've accomplished and achieved; overcome suffering, loss, and adversity; and remain hopeful and encouraged today because God has extended His love, mercy, grace, forgiveness, strength, and power to me! To say that I have "pulled myself up by my bootstraps" or "climbed the social ladder" by my own ingenuity and strength or that my success and fulfillment is a result of being "the captain of my own ship" is like slapping God in the face. I couldn't even breathe if God did not allow me to do so. I would rather walk on a bed of nails than become so vain, unappreciative, and dismissive.

Since I addressed *who* determines whether one is successful and fulfilled, let me address *what* determines success and fulfillment. First let me submit, if success and fulfillment are based on money, fame, and fortune, why are so many wealthy, prominent, popular people in our culture ruining their lives with sex, alcohol, drugs, and reckless living? And if "climbing the social ladder" or "working hard to get to the top" is the recipe for success and fulfillment, why are so many people who've climbed the social ladder or have made it to the top (according to societal standards) depressed, stressed out, greedy, fearful, and lacking true peace—never satisfied and always wanting more?

In my estimation, the answer to the *what* question goes beyond following your own ambitions or accepting a nonspiritual societal view as your best course. There's a greater course humans are designed to follow that goes beyond the human intellect and will. In other words, in answering the *what* question, you must accept the fact that God created us, understands us, and knows the best course for our lives. His purpose, plan, and destiny are the best course this life has to offer. It's the measuring stick for success and fulfillment. Though it can't be argued that you can experience a measure of success and fulfillment in "your own strength" (not really in your own strength because God gives us life, but in terms of following Him), it can't compare to the success and fulfillment found in relationship with Him and doing His will. When we are in harmony with God's plan and destiny for our lives, our potential is maximized and we find meaning, purpose, inspiration, hope, wholeness, and victory beyond our imagination.

Is it easy to pursue God's purpose and plan for your life? Not necessarily. The reason I answered this way is because of the opposition and challenges we face in pursing God's best for our lives. The Bible says we fight against at least three powerful things that attempt to frustrate our efforts in following God's will for our lives. They are the devil, our flesh, and this world. Ephesians 6:11–12; I Peter 5:8; I Peter 2:11; Romans 8:5–7; Romans 12:2; and Colossians 3:2 best illustrate these truths. Observe the following Scriptures.

Put on the whole armor of God, that you may be able to stand against the wiles of the devil. For we do not wrestle against flesh and blood, but against principalities, against powers, against the rulers of the darkness of this age, against spiritual hosts of wickedness in heavenly places (Ephesians 6:11–12).

Be sober, be vigilant; because your adversary the devil walks about like a roaring lion, seeking whom he may devour (I Peter 5:8).

Beloved, I beg you as sojourners and pilgrims, abstain from fleshly lusts which war against your soul (I Peter 2:11).

For those who live according to the flesh set their minds on the things of the flesh, but those who live according to the Spirit, the things of the Spirit. For to be carnally minded is death, but to be spiritually minded is life and peace. Because the carnal mind is enmity against God; for it is not subject to the law of God, nor indeed can be (Romans 8:5–7).

And do not be conformed to this world, but be transformed by the renewing of your mind, that you may prove what is that good and acceptable and perfect will of God (Romans 12:2).

Set your mind on things above, not on things on the earth (Colossians 3:2).

Yes, choosing God's purpose and plan for your life may not be easy. Just because it's not always easy, however, doesn't mean we shouldn't do it. If we don't pursue God's best for our lives, we'll come up short and lose out in the end. Furthermore, Jesus promised us (in St. Matthew 11:30) that "His yoke is easy and His burden is light." Also, the Bible says, "If God be for us, who can be against us," and "we are more than conqueror through Jesus!" (Romans 8:31,37). Therefore, my pursuit and decision to stay on course doesn't have to be easy because God has already made the way for me (and everyone who trust and depend on Him) to succeed and be fulfilled no matter how hard or difficult it gets!

In summation, in living through "The Way It Was" and "The Way It Is" chapters of my journey with loss, God has blessed me to experience "The Way It Can Be" by helping me to grow in faith, service, and life.

God has blessed me to see the value of allowing His grace, mercy, and wisdom to guide me; allowing Him to transform my pain into reaching out and connecting to others; and living by His affirmation and pursuing His destiny for my life. *Living Without Them — My Journey with Loss* is not a journey about loss but victory! Not only has God allowed me to love and celebrate my departed loved ones as long as I shall live, He has used this journey to teach me the greatest truth I know when Jesus said (St. John14:6), "I am the way, the truth, and the life!"

Closing Thoughts

As I wrote the last line of this reflective discourse, I stepped back and thought about the question several people asked me after hearing the title, *Living Without Them — My Journey with Loss:* What's this book (really) about? Although the title does suggest my personal story as it relates to loss, it's so much more! So in these closing thoughts, I'd like to expound upon "what this book is really about" using something similar to the Five W's and H.

Who – Who should read this book? Whereas it's true, I provided a narrative for this journey, everyone (at some point) will have to deal with loss. Therefore, as I reflect upon life before and after a particular loss, how I handled the loss, and what I took away from the loss, I pray that the reader will do the same in reflecting upon his or her journey with loss. As the reader reflects upon his or her life, he or she can discover how "Living Without Them" has impacted his or her life. Questions you might ask yourself are "How do I remember or celebrate my lost loved ones?" "Am I inspired or deflated by their legacy?" "Do I still suffer or am I carrying things from the past that weigh heavily on my heart?" And "How do I allow God to transform my life through these experiences?" Again, this is beyond one's personal story or an individual from a certain background or culture. This is a human journey we all must travel. The question is, will we allow God to make us better or allow life to cause us to be bitter!

What – What's the purpose and goal of the book? Let me start by commenting on what isn't the purpose and goal of the book. This is not a five- or seven-step book on grief and loss. My experience (both personal and in supporting others) in dealing with loss and life is far more complex and challenging than reducing it to "steps" or some man-made formula. As I mentioned in my writings, there are many facets to an individual's situation in dealing with loss, such as the type of personality the person experiencing the loss has; the age of the departed loved one; how close the person was to the departed loved one; how the loved one died—accident, long sickness, murder, old age, etc.; the level of support one has had in dealing with the loss; the departed loved one's beliefs about God, life, and the afterlife; the person's beliefs about these things; and what was going on in one's life at the time of the loss of a loved one. The answer to these types of questions plays a big role in how you process loss. In addition, this book is not about revealing "family secrets" or "exposing weakness." As the Bible proclaims, "For all have sinned and fall short of the glory of God" (Romans 3:23). Rather, this book is about growth, awareness, and progression. It's about owning who you are; where you come from; the important people in your life; how your life is affected when they leave; and how to move forward. It's about loving yourself and those special people in your life in spite of imperfection, instead of perfection. And more importantly, it's about how God can make the difference in your life!

When – When does one stop hurting and start healing? In some ways, this is the "million-dollar question." One definite answer is, it's going to be different for everyone. Another answer is, it's going to depend upon where you are with some of the facets I mentioned in the previous *what* section. In other words, were you very close to this individual, and do you have a good support system in helping you cope with the loss? Did the departed loved one have a belief system and live his or her life in such a way that gives you peace concerning where he or she might spend eternity? Did he or she die of old age or was his or her life cut short? Do you have a relationship with God, and do you pray, read the Bible, meditate on God's promises; fellowship with other believers; and take care of your physical and emotional state of being? Or, do you isolate and push helpful people away? Do you participate in illicit sex, drugs, alcohol, or other self-destructive behaviors to dull the pain? Have you given up on life and become angry, bitter, and lost hope? Suffice to say, you can't (always) control life or control when death knocks on your door. But we can take steps in the right direction that can help us cope with loss and move forward. As we heal, the hurt minimizes and we're transformed into stronger, better people—though the process and the amount of time it takes will vary from person to person.

Where – Where am I now? If life and dealing with loss is a journey and not a destination, then it's imperative that I'm in touch and in tune with myself. I chronicled my life from the time I came into the Tate family until I retired from the Air Force because it's important to know what was going on in my life before, during, and after my experiences with loss. I'm one of those individuals who wants to know how I tick and how I've gotten from point A to Z. For me, it's very hard to know where you are unless you know where you've been; how the past might affect the present; and where you hope to go in the future. However, I would never advocate the reader limit the scope of this book to discovering where Jose is—that's too small. The gift of hearing someone's journey is to rethink and ask the question, Where am I? Am I broken? Do I need God's healing or restoration? Do I have hope today? Am I able to move forward? I pray that these questions are raised for the reader to process as you take my spiritual journey and journey with loss into consideration.

Why – Why write this book? This book was born out of ministry. On several occasions when I worked with individuals dealing with life issues and loss, I would share "pieces" of my story—when appropriate—

to connect, but never to shift the focus from parishioner/client/patient to minister/chaplain. As individuals heard these "pieces" of my story, several became encouraged and hopeful that they could overcome and move forward as well. In addition, family and friends encouraged me to write a book about my journey. At first, I didn't put much stock in writing this kind of book. Eventually, I felt that if my story could help someone, then it would be worth telling. I must admit, I didn't fully realize what I was getting myself into. Not only did it take a long time to complete, I didn't expect to experience some "powerful moments" as I reflected on the journey. Was it personally satisfying to put my journey on paper? Yes, but it was a little challenging at times. Nevertheless, I kept thinking about the individual out there in the world who's going through similar things and who hungers for inspiration. My message is be inspired that we have a God who cares; is able to reach us where we are; and is able to give us a new, fresh perspective on life and loss as we relate to Him.

How – How does one move from loss to victory? Although this question may seem similar to the *when* question, there's a subtle difference. When I think about hurt and healing, I think about the "emotional" side of dealing with loss in terms of how I "feel." I've heard people say (and I've said it as well in my life), I "feel" like people don't understand what I'm going through, even though there were empathetic people around attempting to show some love. On the other hand, when one experiences loss, there's no denying that it happened. But the loss doesn't have to define one's life or dictate the choices one makes in moving forward. In other words, emotionally, I may hurt from experiencing a loss, but I'm victorious in terms of "The Way It Can Be" for me. I have not surrendered or given power to the situation to negatively impede my life and cause me to stay stuck or move backward in life. For me, moving from loss to victory always includes God.

Whether God is working behind the scenes or out in front, God helps you cope, heal, grow, and move forward better than anything else in the universe. Not only does God help you to "Live Without Them," He helps you to honor, celebrate, and keep their legacy alive!

Made in the USA
Monee, IL
31 October 2023